YOU COULDN'T MAKE THIS UP

REAL STORIES
REAL LIFE

You Couldn't Make This Up

Ellie Searl
Carolyn B Healy
Mary Lou Edwards

ISBN 13:   9781452810607
ISBN 10:   1452810605
LCCN: 2010921832

WATER TOWER PRESS
CHICAGO, ILLINOIS

PRINTED IN THE USA

DEDICATED TO ...

. . . the characters in my stories . . .
I've enjoyed your company.
~ Ellie ~

. . . David, Ben, and Katy - the best.
~ Carolyn ~

. . . Raphael, Coco, and Olivia, who snoozed at my feet many a
night while I burned the midnight oil.
. . . And to George and Lia, who read and reread, and read again,
the fruits of my labor.
~ MLE ~

CONTENTS

CONTENTS

READERS' FAVORITES
FROM
LITTLE DID WE KNOW:
MAKING THE WRITE IMPRESSION

IN BETWEEN

You cannot hope to build a better world without improving individuals. To that end, each of us must work for our own improvement, and, at the same time, share a general responsibility for all humanity, our particular duty being to aid those to whom we think we can be most useful.

~ Madame Marie Curie ~

THE SLEEPING BABY

Mary Lou Edwards

Girls didn't get kicked out of school.

Even boys didn't get kicked out of school unless they were totally incorrigible, and incorrigible was loosely defined.

Bean the Fiend practically killed someone with a baseball bat, and he didn't even get suspended. They said it was because the guy he almost murdered was colored, and colored people were not supposed to come into Bridgeport so he was really asking for it. But my dad said no human being deserved such treatment, and the incident was a dirty shame. Nothing happened to Bean, and he should have been history.

Joey the Nut torched someone's garage: he wasn't expelled either. The grapevine had it that graduation was only a couple of weeks away so the nuns didn't want to bother, but I suspected they were worried the convent would go up in flames if they dared get rid of him.

Two criminals skated, and the nuns wanted to throw me out?

The day before, Sister Margaret Anne, my six foot, seventh grade teacher, who sported more than a bit of a mustache, had clomped over to my desk in her huge black wing-tips and handed me an envelope. "Give this to your parents," she barked. "I want to see them as soon as possible."

In the days before teacher conferences were routine, when dads worked double shifts, when moms made tri-colored Jell-O molds and baked cookies from scratch, having your mother, never mind both parents, called to school was equivalent to an executioner's drum roll.

The night of the doomsday meeting, I sat at the kitchen table preparing myself for something awful. My parents came home: I read their faces and the message was not good.

"You finally did it," my father announced as he hung up his jacket and pulled out a chair. He and my mother had just returned from the dreaded meeting. "You got yourself thrown out." Lowering his voice so as not to wake my sister, he continued, "Yes, the nuns have finally had enough of your big mouth. They want you gone - out of there - by the end of the school year. Shaking his head and raising his eyebrows with a you-just-never-learn look, he added, "I've told you a million times to watch your step."

"Jim, stop it," my mother said as she put the dinner dishes in the cabinet.

I could not believe Mom was not freaked out at a time like this. Apparently, she'd yet to realize my disgrace would instantly qualify her for The Mothers Who Failed Hall of Shame.

My heart was thumping; I thought my pajama top would fly up in my face. I knew my father was not joking because he had almost no sense of humor plus he had warned me, "Your smart mouth will get you in trouble one day. Mark my words." It was clear that a girl who spoke out had a major problem. Sooner or later, she was guaranteed her Waterloo.

But this seemed so drastic.

True, I had gotten more than my share of checkmarks in kindergarten, but, for the most part, I had cleaned up my act. Gone was the girl who would not put her head down on her desk and rest quietly, wait her turn patiently at lavatory time or play well with others. I still had a few flaws, but not enough to warrant banishment. My grades were excellent. I wasn't perfect, but, unlike a lot of the troublemakers in my room, I never had to put money in the Mission Box for The Pagan Babies in China.

OK, so I finished my assignments lickety-split and spent time whispering and passing notes until the slow-pokes were done with their work. But I was also the one who helped other kids diagram sentences and drilled them on the state capitals. This was my thank-you for grading all of Sister's spelling tests every week, for putting all the arithmetic problems on the blackboard every morning? This was my reward for spending my daily recess down in first grade dressing the brats who couldn't even tell their right boot from their left? Would they really dump their star funeral mass singer who chanted countless dirges whenever another parishioner kicked the bucket?

My mother, noting the shock waves of disbelief and anger roll cross my face, intervened.

"Jim, stop this nonsense," she insisted. "Tell her the truth." My mom was trying to pull me in off the ledge my father was greasing.

As she stood at the sink filling Skippy's water bowl, she said, "You are being double promoted because of some test your class took. Your scores were very high."

"You don't really believe that, do you, Mary?" my dad interrupted. "She's a giant pain and they want her out of their hair."

Just before the meeting, my mother had taken a cake out of the oven and now she put it on the table. She believed food always made things better.

"Yes, they're sick of putting up with her," he continued, while I sat there totally bewildered. "Sister didn't want to be blunt, but I could read between the lines. She was trying to be nice."

"No, that's not true," my mother shot back, cutting an extra big piece of chocolate cake for me. "Daddy's just saying that because he doesn't want you to think who *you are*. He doesn't want you to get a big head," my mom whispered, as though this all made perfect sense.

Was my father practicing his version of that old Italian adage about only kissing sleeping babies? If you kissed a baby when she was awake, she might think she was really special, really important, and, God forbid, think *Who. She. Was.*

Sensing my confusion and getting impatient with this mind-game, my mother picked up the empty plates and put them in the sink. "Listen to me. Sister Benedict said you need to be challenged. On Monday, you'll go to 8th grade for two months and then graduate. Now get to bed. It's late."

The drama was over, just like that. No one asked if this was something I'd like to do or what did I think. No discussion, just get to bed.

The thumping of my heart subsided, but the spinning in my head had only just begun. The master of mixed messages had added another chapter, *Planting the Seeds of Self-Doubt,* to his best-seller **HOW TO DESTROY YOUR KID'S CONFIDENCE.**

For graduation I was given an Art Nouveau wristwatch with a tiny diamond on each corner of its beautiful hinged platinum case. The square white-gold face had small, swirly Arabic numerals at 12, 3, 6, and 9. My mother confided that she'd objected to the expense, but my dad told her my present had to be really special to show me how pleased they were of my achievement. Why couldn't he have told me that? Why couldn't he just say, "Your mother and I are really proud of you."

And then it occurred to me that, maybe as a baby, he'd only been kissed when he was sleeping.

YOU CAN'T ALWAYS GET
WHAT YOU WANT

Carolyn B Healy

My high school was one of the best in the Chicago Public School system – academically superior, racially stable, with a host of after-school activities. A substantial percentage of students went on to college. It had the customary social divisions for the time: the cool kids, the hoody kids and the nerds, even though that word was not in use yet. Everyone pretty much knew where they belonged, but our school had a particularly vivid way of drawing the distinctions, at least for the white kids.

The black kids must have had their own stratification, but in our self-involvement, we got only a glimpse. Within our honors classes, there was a bit of a range from the ultra studious twins, to the hardworking activity jock who ran the yearbook, to the glamorous girl who belted out the theme from *Goldfinger* at the talent show. We were school-friends, but never met outside of school, and never wondered why.

My drama played out on the border between the cool kids and everyone else. *There* were three sororities that exercised considerable power over the social structure not to mention our own fragile self-definitions. The first was for the upper crust girls. Prosperous, attractive, socially adept, they occupied the top rung of the social ladder, and no surprise, included most of the cheerleaders, the true elite. We'll call them Group A, though they had a fancy three-Greek-letter name.

Group B was at the other extreme, the girls who were tougher, more likely to come from blue collar families, less concerned with the social niceties, less active in school activities or currying favor with teachers. The hoody girls.

Group C was in the middle, the regular girls, nice, smart, busy with activities. I aspired to Group C.

On one level I knew better. I objected in principle to the concept of excluding girls based on some secret and specious measurement of their adequacy. But I was so entranced by the prospect of converting my outsider status (no father, no siblings) to become one who belonged, I abandoned my principles and went through rush, along with nearly all my friends.

The separation began right there. The nice plain girl with the white blouse and circle pin didn't even try. And the quiet and socially awkward girl who sat near me in class stayed home too. I barely noticed. It was almost my birthday and I knew what I wanted this year. My new life was about to begin.

I remember nothing about the rush parties, but I think they involved punch and cookies and favors. I remember bid night perfectly. From my second floor apartment, sitting at my desk overlooking the intersection of 111th Street and Hoyne, I watched with excitement for the Group C car to pull up and bring me my invitation to join. The minutes ticked by.

When I saw the car approach, and then go whizzing on by, I realized that my big chance had vanished in their dust. I think I got on the phone with my best friend who was also awaiting her fate, but I couldn't swear to it. I might have been mute with shame.

By the end of the night, it was clear that she was without a bid too. It seemed less tragic that way and we soon rose to the occasion, declaring ourselves GDIs – God Damned Independents. I think we even made up GDI sweatshirts. It was only spring of sophomore year after all, and we had to construct some sort of social identity that would see us through the coming three years.

All our friends pledged Group C and were soon wearing pledge ribbons, attending meetings and receiving orders to bake chocolate chip cookies and deliver them to the house of this or that "active." With the cookies and other demands, it started to dawn on me that I might not have been very well suited to pledgehood anyway. I had better things to do than bake other people cookies.

The only friend who deviated joined Group B, the one her sister belonged to. She and I always walked to school together, so I saw her toting her cookie orders and watched her sister's friend ordering her around. She didn't seem to be having that much fun.

Two weeks later another friend, a successful Group C pledge, invited me over for Saturday night. She said that she invited some other girls too. Just what I needed, I thought, a respite from the social anguish of the past days. I got dropped off, walked into her living room, and was engulfed by 12 girls yelling, "Happy Birthday." They gave me a huge homemade card and a cake. And the most therapeutic surprise I've ever had.

We had such fun that we decided to meet again and again for what we came to call hen parties. We named ourselves The Crew and drank Diet Rite, ate shortbread cookies and had more fun than anyone.

The months went by, and rush season came around again. I put my hat in the ring again, generously providing Group C the opportunity to correct their mistake. Once again, they declined.

I did get visits that bid night from the other two. I sensed that Group A was quite certain that I would gratefully take them up on it. And that Group B was motivated by respect for my walking-to-school friend who must have urged them to include me. It must have been that, because we all knew that I was a goody-two-shoes who couldn't begin to keep up with the tougher girls in Group B.

What did I do? The most contrary thing I could. I turned down Group A, explaining that I didn't feel I would fit in, silently enjoying their disbelief. I accepted Group B in thanks to my friend and their willingness to accept an unusual candidate. I dropped out within a week, on the eve of my first cookie order. She understood.

By then, half of my Crew friends had grown weary of the indignities they'd suffered as pledges, and the painful process of rush. One dropped out of Group C, others barely attended their meetings, and one ended up president. We each found our own way.

In the gifts where you least expect them department, The Crew has lived on to be a sustaining force in my life ever since that 15th year birthday party. We're meeting at Estes Park this summer, and will continue until we conk out for good. I sure didn't get what I wanted, but ended up with so much more than I imagined.

SEARCHING FOR SIGNAL

Ellie Searl

The older couple sat beside me in Row Three - wife in the middle; husband at the window.

Her head looked like a camel molting in late spring. Sparse patches of short, reddish-brown dyed hair with muddy grey roots rose from her scalp in clumps - a bald spot highlighted her crown. She wore a turquoise polyester pants suit, sensible brown shoes with Velcro straps, and lots of costume jewelry.

He matched his wife's lackluster style - tousled grey hair, lumpy beige suit, tan tie shoes. He slumped so far into his seat I couldn't see his face. He mumbled something.

"They're down there." She pointed to a pink, quilted bag under the seat in front of her.

"Huh?"

"They're there. . . In that bag. . . down there. . . !"

"WHAT?"

He reminded me of my father - asking a question but oblivious to it when it was answered.

I could hear them shout at each other over the roar of the Jet Blue engine and my headphones, which were already turned up several notches so I could watch "Real Housewives of Orange County" on the little TV above my tray table. The title of that show is a misnomer. Reality shows like OC Housewives don't reflect real anything. They're orchestrated and semi-scripted by the producers to titillate the audience with exaggerated drama, turmoil, and superficial, yo-yo relationships of fatuous non-actors. Seldom in real life are people's everyday activities packed with such absurd behaviors and outrageous upheavals as those represented by these OC women, at least not in my experience. I don't really approve of the show, but it's fun to watch with my daughter for the ridicule factor, and I figured it would be good entertainment for part of my four-hour plane trip back to Chicago.

"I . . . SAID . . . YES! . . . I BROUGHT THE SNACKS!"

The flight attendant looked at our row. She moved toward us just as a tall, thin woman shot into the galley, arms flailing, head thrust forward, spewing something at the attendant with such intensity I thought she needed medical attention. Her outfit screamed *pay attention to me*: tilted black beret, wide-rimmed jeweled sunglasses, fur-lined leather vest, skin-tight shirt and jeans, fringed brown suede boots, and a gold metal purse slung over her shoulder. The attendant held up a snack package and they studied the back. Just some diet issue. Apparently satisfied, the long-limbed woman returned to her seat in the back of the plane.

"WELL, GET 'EM OUT."

An armful of bracelets clanked as my seatmate extricated her bag from the metal rungs. She hefted it with an audible "umph," trying to keep it from toppling back onto her feet.

"Help me hold onto this thing."

"HUH?"

"I said. . . HELP. ME. WITH. THIS. THING!"

I tried to concentrate on the OC Housewives with their annoying outbursts and communication breakdowns. The scene I was watching had Vicki telling her husband, Don, that he wasn't allowed to accompany her and her children from a previous marriage on their annual Mexican vacation because, *"It's always been a tradition that it's just me and the kids."* Of course, Don's feels left out, and Vicki tells him to *"Get over it,"* but then she tells the audience that Don doesn't fill her 'love tank.' There are times I feel compelled to shout at TV, and this was one of them. *"Do you hear yourself - you sniveling, narcissistic twit?"*

"PUT THE DAMN THING DOWN FOR CHRIST'S SAKE!" He slammed his hand on his knee.

The lady plopped the bag onto our shared armrest, grumbling something about 'always complaining.' She unzipped the bag and dumped the contents - bananas, juice boxes, baggies of peanut butter crackers, pretzels, goldfish, raisins, caramels - into her lap . . . and into mine. I returned her bananas, snacks, and a leaking juice box.

"Oh, I'm sorry, dear. Here let me get that." Her bracelets rattled as she yanked a wadded tissue from under her cuff and began to mop juice drippings off my fingers.

"Really, it's fine," I told her, pulling my hand away from her and her used Kleenex. I turned up the volume on my headset.

She leaned toward her husband. **"What do you want to eat?"**

"WHAT?"

"WHAT...DO ... YOU...WANT...? BANANA? JUICE? CANDY? WADDA YA WANT? *Geeze, what a pill."*

The mystery woman charged through the cabin, parked her chin in front of the flight attendant, wagged a finger back and forth an inch from the attendant's nose, and pointed down the aisle spouting something with such acrimony I knew it didn't concern the nutritional values of sweet potato chips. The attendant maintained a calm demeanor, but her furtive glances indicated she was reconnoitering escape routes. After a few minutes of the harangue, the irate passenger huffed her way to the back of the plane. I was sorry I couldn't hear this verbal exchange. I figured it would have been far more fascinating than the one beside me.

"GIMME A BANANA."

"YOU WANT ME TO PEEL IT, TOO?"

She ripped at the stem, but he grabbed it before she could pull it down.
I looked around to see who else noticed this confluence of noise and activity in the front of the plane. But most travelers were otherwise occupied – reading, watching TV, sleeping.

She fussed with the snacks. "You know, Jack can be so demanding sometimes. *'Gimme this, gimme that.'* Can't hear a word I'm saying. Should have seen him try to get through security. I told him to take off his shoes. He knew he was supposed to take off his shoes. I told him before we left the house he'd have to take off his shoes."

I stared at TV, hoping it would discourage the shoe commentary. It didn't.

"Did he wear shoes he could take off? No. What does he wear? He wears those stupid tie shoes. He can barely bend over to tie 'em the first place. Has to sit down to tie his shoes. I told him to wear the shoes with the Velcro straps. Like mine." She lifted her left foot and pointed. "Now, I wore *my* shoes with the Velcro straps. See, they're easy to get on and off. I wear 'em everywhere – even to the Doctor's office. Did he wear his? No. He had to wear tie shoes. Didn't hear a word the security man said to him. *'TAKE OFF YOUR SHOES!'* We kept shouting at him. *'TAKE OFF YOUR SHOES!'* Lord, I wish he'd just go to sleep. Would you like a snack?" She held up a bag of raisins.

"No, no, thanks. I'm just going to watch a little TV and then take a nap."
I turned my attention back to OC Housewives. Vicki and Don were at a fancy restaurant. Vicki wiped her eyes with her cloth napkin. *"I need to know you love me. Can't you tell me you love me?"*

I felt a hand on my arm. "Where are you going, honey? You live in Chicago? Our daughter lives in Chicago. Not the city. The suburbs. She just had a baby. Girl. Named her Colby. Can you imagine? Naming a baby after a cheese? I hate to say it, but the poor kid looks like a squirrel. You like Chicago? Jack hates Chicago. I don't know why he bothered to come this time. You sure you don't want something to eat? Here. Have a banana."

"No, really. I'm not hungry," I lied. I was very hungry, but I didn't want to share iffy food packed under doubtful circumstances by people who thought bananas on a plane were appetizing and called their baby grand-daughter a squirrel.

High-maintenance lady sped by in a rage. **"Why the *Hell* hasn't someone found me a *fucking* better seat?** *Christ!* **What do I have to do? Kick some *asshole* out *myself?*"**

In a swift second, three flight attendants swooped around her next to my row. "Ma'am, we've already told you. There are no more available seats. I'm sorry, but you'll have to remain where you are. What is the problem with it?"

"Well, it's next to a *baby*, and . . . and . . . I don't like your *rhetoric!*"

"I'll move!" I shouted at them without thinking. The aisle confab looked at me, startled into silence. I lowered my voice. "I'd be more than happy to switch seats. Please, sit here."

And without giving anyone time to refuse, I gathered my things, stood up, and waited for new seat instructions. My seatmate looked baffled. "You okay, dear? Can I help? . . . You're . . . *leaving?*"

The last thing I heard on TV before I took off my headset was Jeana trashing the 'new girl' - *"She's lucky she didn't get bitch-slapped!"*

JOURNEY

People take different roads seeking fulfillment and happiness.
Just because they're not on
your road doesn't mean they've gotten lost.

~ H. Jackson Brown, Jr. ~

A CHILL IN CUBA

Carolyn B Healy

The scene –
Hotel lobby, Havana:

• A polished wooden bar ringed with rattan stools, bathed in soft light

• Polished mosaic tables arranged at the base of a spectacular marble staircase; a wide balcony overlooks the entire lobby

• Potted tropical plants sit everywhere

• A guitar player roams from table to table

The main characters –
Five American travelers:

• My husband David and me, who can best be described as touristy looking Midwesterners

• Our two new trip friends, Sue, a gentle 70 year-old former bank CFO who looks about 45 and her wisecracking friend Linda, who could also pass for 10 or 20 years younger than she is

• Matt, late 20's, the baby of our humanitarian tour group, as all the other travelers are 30 to 50 years his senior. His gelled hair and dark blue eyes make him stand out from the other young people in the lobby, as does his formal Southern gentleman manner.

The supporting cast:

• An amiable bartender who shows off a bit in the production of his drinks and engages customers in pleasant banter, just like your local bartender at home

• A cranky expressionless waitress upon whom it seems lost that she has one of the best jobs in Cuba, in that she works in a ritzy spot where she can receive tips in CUC's, the dollar-like currency usually reserved for foreigners

• A fluid assortment of other patrons, all Europeans and Canadians, sampling cigars and local drinks

Tipoff that you are in Havana:

• Solemn business-suited guards stand at various stations on the balcony, surveying the scene. Every half hour they rotate.

• At first we figure that they are watching us. We eventually learn that we are of little interest. They really watch their fellow Cubans, with good reason. With the black market about the only part of the economy that's thriving, just about every commodity, from toilet paper to bathrobes to eggs, apparently tries to walk out the back door.

• That, and the housekeeping staff being dressed in French maid outfits. They don't even have those in France anymore from what I've seen. Although this hotel started out as a joint venture with the Dutch, and they may know things that I don't. Actually, it was that until the Dutch bailed out, one year in, finding the flow of items out the back door untenable when it came to making a profit, kind of an unfamiliar concept in Cuba. So Cuba's former colonial oppressor Spain came through to take over for the Dutch, suggesting that they either have greater risk tolerance or a tougher protocol to keep an eye on the goods.

Opening scene:

David and I enter the lobby, back from an evening stroll through Parque Central, a large tree-lined square across the street. Sue and Linda wave us over to their table where they enjoy Mulatas, Cuban specialty drinks personally prepared by our featured bartender. They launch into stories about the friend of a friend who they spent the afternoon with, an American woman married to a Cuban musician. We try to get the attention of the surly waitress who stares at a boisterous group of German tourists instead.

Lurching past the table comes young Matt, apparently over-served again as he had been at the opening night welcome party. He slows, raises a hand in greeting and lands in our empty chair. It is unclear whether that was his intention or the result of impaired balance.

"Would you like to join us?" Sue asks, a little late.

He looks from right to left, as fast as his depressed central nervous system can manage, and finds no way out. "Sure, I'll have a drink with you. What're ya having?" he asked, eyeing the Mulatas.

He snaps his fingers in the air and the snappish waitress appears at his elbow. "We'll have a round of...these," he said lifting Sue's drink as an example, "Honey." Eager to see how she would show her displeasure, we all turn in time to see her smile warmly at him.

Matt, incapable of multitasking at the moment, pauses in order to concentrate on her departing rump. We watch him watch her until she reaches the bar.

The story unfolds:

"So Matt," Linda says, "How is it that you are here? Are those people we saw you with at the party your parents?"

In the next 20 minutes we learn that:

• He was not related to the couple. "We are not traveling together. We are just on the same trip." What?

• They did have a connection. "We are both pilots." Pause for effect. "He is my friend." The man in question was a handsome fast-moving fellow who didn't say much, but seemed like a solid citizen. Matt acknowledged that the man and his wife had taken him under their wing, leaving us to wonder why he needed that protection.

• Every night he trolled Cuban night spots until 4am. "It makes it a bitch to make the bus," which left every morning at 8 to transport us to the day's activities.

• He was reluctant to say how he made his living except that it involved his plane and the Caribbean. "Well, this and that. I couldn't go to a job in a suit. I'd have to shoot myself." He did look spiffy in a crisp Hawaiian shirt and pleated khakis straight out of wardrobe for Miami Vice.

• His parents had disappointed him in a major way. "Well, my mom, let's just say she's out of my life. And my dad. They went to New York. I'm an orphan." That sent my writer's imagination flipping through death, divorce, suicide, abuse - wait, I think that's my therapist's imagination. He waved off further questions.

• He was enraptured with the Cuban people, the ones he was meeting in his nightly forays. "You meet such fabulous people out there. You have to get out of here to do it. They don't let them in here you know." We did know that Raul, having taken over from Fidel some months before, had quickly changed the policy that allowed no Cubans in hotels unless they worked there. Fidel's reasoning: Why let people limping along on ration cards see how other people live, unless they work there and benefit from it; not to mention the prostitution thing. Raul's: What the heck? Let them live a little. Besides, they can't afford it. The Cuban pesos they get paid in don't spend there.

His popularity with the Cubans he was meeting - was it his personality, looks, CUC's? Was he being courted for what he would be willing to do? He invited David to accompany him that night. He declined, partly because it was past his bedtime, partly out of good radar for trouble.

Matt made every effort to turn on the charm, but the attempt fell flat except for his effect on the waitress. He employed the disorienting lack of eye contact that makes you look over your shoulder to see what he's really looking at - and find that there's nothing there. Again, this raised the question of whether this was intentional or a temporary alcohol-induced inability to focus.

The conversation stayed all about him, with our complicity, each of us throwing in leading questions to keep him going, hoping we'd hit a vein of authenticity if we dug hard enough.

I began to develop a chill, the same chill I've felt when I've met people over the years, clients and others, who consider harm to others or themselves an acceptable risk if it allows them to get what they want – thrills, revenge, financial gain, whatever. That chill comes from being in the presence of a person who just might do anything.

What was he up to? Gun-running, drugs, unauthorized immigration, whatever he was told? Or was it just posing, an attempt to inflate an underdeveloped self?

He rose, attempting gallantry, "It's been a pleasure..."

We let him go and resumed our talk about what Sue and Linda had learned in their afternoon trip to real Havana.

A few minutes later, we noticed him back at the bar, a new drink and giant cigar in hand, leaning over two blonde tourists, a hand on each of their shoulders.

"Bond," I said, "James Bond." We called him James Junior after that, or Junior for short. We shared our speculations about his actual business and motives, and concluded that we were just glad he wasn't our kid, drifting untethered in a sea of potential trouble.

As Matt stooped lower to talk more intimately into the girls' faces, David said, "I'll tell you this - he's not going to be able to consummate whatever he starts tonight. Guaranteed." Our pals whooped, a little scandalized, and we retreated back into discussion of the packages of clothespins their friend had requested and how she planned to barter them for other rarities like eggs and milk, with one of the front desk receptionists she had befriended among others.

We broke up after a nightcap and retreated to our luxurious rooms with marble and bathrobes and a view of the formerly grand buildings now trending toward slums, and continued to try to make sense of Cuba, where people seemed so like us and the world they lived in so different. And wondered about Matt's world, where with any luck, we would never have to visit again.

CRAYON CIGARETTES

Ellie Searl

Wild-eyed Sally waved the serrated bread knife in front of Ed's face. I could see her through the crack in the kitchen door. Her untamed hair flew around and she spat venom. "If she comes in here, I'll kill her. I hate her guts, and she better watch out!"

Ed knew how to handle Sally. He remained calm. "Sally, give me the knife. . ."

She made small jabbing motions toward his throat. "I hate her! She's a pig! How can you stand her?"

"You don't mean that." His voice softened. "Do you really want to hurt Ellie?"

She backed off, heaving the knife to the floor. It clatter-bounced on the tile and skittered under the stove.

Sally was part Cree, part French Canadian, part Scottish, and part unknown. I'm not sure which part of her wanted to kill me – probably all of it. She was thirteen, tall, skinny, abandoned by her family, secretly in love with Ed, and mad. She was mad at me because I wouldn't let her go out. It was a weekday – a school night. The girls weren't allowed out after supper on school nights. Not Cindy, not Carol, not Ellen, not Leez, not Tony, not Lauren, and not Sally - especially not Sally, who didn't understand her emotions and couldn't control an ounce of them.

A few weeks earlier, when Sally and I had been on better terms, we all sat in the living room wondering what our collective lives would be like after Ed finished theological school and we left the group home. Ed casually declared, "Sally, if you want me to, I'll marry you."

Sally's cheeks turned apple red and her face slowly transformed from horror-struck to befuddlement to glee to utter and complete triumph. Without moving her head, she ping-ponged glances from Ed to me. Then under a cupped hand, asked Ed in a throaty whisper, "But what about Ellie?" Sally was devastated to learn that Ed would only officiate at a ceremony where she would marry someone probably most unwelcome at this time in her unfortunate teenage life.

My assistant, Carly, charged up from the basement. "What's going on? Who's screaming?"

"It's Sally. I won't let her go out, so she's going to kill me - again."

"Oh, ok, with a knife?"

"Yeah - would you check on Leez? I think she's chanting. Make sure her door's closed."

Carol stuck her head out of her room *"Sally! Leez! Shut – the – hell – up!"*

Our daughter, Katie, stood at the top of the stairs clutching her blanket and stuffed baby weasel. "Mommy, I can't sleep. Is Sally going to kill you? Leez is making a funny sound in her room. And Carol just said a bad word."

"Let's get you back to bed. We'll read a story."

Life in the group home was chaotic, to say the least. At any given time, there were twelve people living, eating, sleeping, cooking, cleaning, studying, or screaming in the house - seven female teenage wards of the state, two house parents with a four-year-old daughter, one live-in college student assistant, and a Caribbean housekeeper, Inez, who was a better cook than a cleaner.

By the time Sally wanted to kill me, Ed and I had been house parents for the United Red Feather Services of Greater Montreal for almost two years. Our house was a duplex in Montreal West converted into a one-family dwelling. The main floor had a living room, a dining room, two bedrooms, a full bathroom, and a long kitchen in the back that stretched the width of the house. The upstairs had the same configuration, with all five main rooms turned into bedrooms, including the kitchen. The basement had a finished family room and laundry.

Our room was on the main floor, so we could monitor daily activity, and Katie's room was the kitchen-turned- bedroom upstairs. Hers was a nice space - cupboards for books, toys, and games, a sink for privacy, and a quiet balcony for us to sit in the sun and color and read stories away from the turbulence of broken teenage girls, who would still be on the road to emotional and physical bankruptcy had the Quebec juvenile justice system not stepped in and placed them in a strange home where they were expected to coexist in peace, friendship, and harmony, regardless of the heartbreaking reasons they had been removed from their dangerous homes.

How did two years in this house of turmoil affect Katie's psyche? She has never complained, but I'm sure there is a part of her that recalls the heartache and desperation that spread around her like air-dust floating in the sun, seeping into her being as she breathed. What lingers in Katie's now married, mother-heart that unconsciously resonates to the haunting memory of late night, hollow sobbing? Is there a residual empathy that serves her children or husband more compassionately because at such a tender age she witnessed the disenfranchisement of young women tossed from household to household? Does she watch over her little boy more intently? Hold her little girl more securely? Will she over-smooth their paths so they won't stumble?

These were not areas of concern when we agreed to feed, supervise, and nurture seven troubled teenage girls for pay. We were a young family who needed a home and occupation while Ed finished theological school at McGill University. I received a full-time salary for serving as house mother and Ed received a part-time salary as house father. We paid no rent, and except for our car, all of our expenses, including food, were handled by the agency. It seemed perfect when we accepted the job. No one mentioned the havoc that would gradually erode our spirits.

Leez opened the door to her room. *"Shiiiiittttttttt on you all! Shit! Shit! Shit! Shit! Shit!"* Leez had stopped chanting and, instead, regaled the house with obscenities. Her profanity was usually more creative than a one-word shit repetition. I figured her level of frustration was so high she couldn't dredge up the usual vulgar repertoire. *"Shit and shit on you all."*

I knew Leez would continue swearing in the hallway until someone met her face-to-face and told her to stop, at which time she'd snigger and say something ridiculous, like, "I need a hairbrush." Leez sought attention by screeching, and all my effective methods as an experienced disciplinarian couldn't make a dent in her shriek-clad armor. Even the director of Red Feather agency had to admit she was truly impossible after he took her for a weekend to prove he could handle her better than we did – but she was unmanageable even with him, and short of electric shock treatments, Leez would remain an unpredictable pain in the neck. I felt vindicated, but that didn't stop Leez from turning our already crazy household upside down whenever she wanted anything.

The house continued to reverberate with screams and threats as Katie and I settled in to read her favorite Maurice Sendak book - WHERE THE WILD THINGS ARE - 'The night Max wore his wolf suit, and made mischief of one kind and another, his mother called him Wild Thing.'

"Max was like Sally and Leez," Katie whispered as she turned the page.

I tried to explain to Katie why the girls behaved as they did even though she had no reference points. I wanted Katie to understand, at least a little bit, that Ellen hid food and dirty underpants in a trunk at the foot of her bed because throughout her abused, miserable fourteen years, she never had anything to call her own, or that Cindy was disrespectful and sarcastic because she didn't trust I'd care about her for more than two seconds, or that Tony was afraid we'd beat her senseless for nothing more than forgetting to hang up her coat, like her dad did when he broke her arm before the authorities placed her in foster care, or that Lauren cried herself to sleep every night because her twin sister was placed in a different group home across town and hardly ever saw her, or that Carol, the oldest, most mature, most reliable of the bunch, might not ever get over the debilitating grief she carried since her boyfriend, Jack, drowned the summer before after shooting himself up with heroin and diving off a cliff into the St. Lawrence River.

But Katie never judged the girls. She just wanted to imitate them or play games with them or watch them gossip and bicker. Katie smoked her crayons to be like Ellen. She liked her long, curly blonde hair to look like Carol's - twisted into a floppy knot and decorated with ribbons and plastic barrettes. She sat next to Cindy during study time, writing repetitive loops page after page on her steno pad, and she read Lauren's big books upside down in the dark.

Sally stormed up the stairs and pounded on Katie's door. *"Get out here, you bitch!"*

I told Katie not to worry; Sally loved her and Daddy and me and nothing bad would happen. What made me so sure, I have no idea. There was little evidence that anyone would be ok in that house, with its exposed, sparking wires of rage, disappointment, resentment, and revenge hanging over us ready to collapse at any moment. Today, under the same circumstances, I'd have my cell phone and pager with me and maybe even wear a medical alert necklace. *"Help! I'm pinned down by a crazed teenager and I can't get up!"* But at the time, I had confidence in my ability to maneuver around the hazards.

I stepped outside Katie's room and shut the door. Sally's squinted at me. Her arms were crossed, and she tapped her foot as if she were about to scold me for stealing cookies. She had no knife.

I merely said, "Sally, I know you're angry, and that's ok." I walked past her, checking in my imaginary rear view mirror that she didn't open Katie's door. Sally stormed into the room she shared with Leez to continue their rants in private. That was the last I heard from either of them that night.

Ed and I did the best we could to help the girls navigate carefully through this tumultuous phase of their lives. Even Katie held their hands on bumpy sidewalks. But we couldn't help them traverse the years back to their little-girl days to celebrate those long-past milestones - losing a first tooth, entering Kindergarten, finding a firefly, sitting on Santa's lap, or graduating from eighth grade. These childhood high points could have fostered trust, poise, security, and a sense of self-worth had they been noticed and commemorated.

All children deserve safe travel into adulthood. Unconditional love, absolute support, steadfast encouragement, and good will are their rights along the way. Rough roads and potholes are expected, but many children, instead, encounter more severe roadblocks: black ice, falling rocks, and dead ends – making the chances of safe passage negligible. If only these children could look over the map ahead of time and use their innocent, unsullied love and wisdom to mark their own routes into the future.

DON'T WE ALL AND HAVEN'T WE ALWAYS

Mary Lou Edwards

When I write about my father, the picture painted can be harsh. It was a thorny relationship, I joked, because we were twins born thirty-three years apart - mirror images who shared generous hearts and quick minds, but also iron wills and fierce tempers - a volatile combination. Perhaps a lithograph, where oil and water don't mix, better describes the bond, but I prefer heavy oils, which never fade.

All paintings require contrast and balance, emphasis, proportion, perspective. No small task to see a picture when one is in it, distance oneself when love blurs the vision, or appreciate a child's worm's-eye view for what it is - justified, but limited.

The brush of humor blends rough lines, the stroke of wit softens glaring reality but, without perspective, the finished product is one-dimensional, without texture or shape. Creating the illusion of three dimensions by applying layers of heavy oil, scraped from the palette of emotion with tints of laughter and shades of hurt, is no substitute. Though impaired eyesight was corrected early on - I wore eyeglasses from third grade - it would take much longer for me to recognize my heart's limited perception, clouded by circumstance, distorted by pain.

Age, however, changed my vision, allowed me to fly above the landscape, to get a bird's-eye view of a sub-culture, which rigidly defined the male role as man of the house, breadwinner, ruler of the roost and king of the castle. A culture that not only accepted certain behaviors, but expected and required them as well. A culture that revered rules, and valued authority over expression - where shame and fear kept people in line - where life was serious, tough, leaving no room for mistakes, risks or wrong moves - where there were no second chances.

New lenses improved my mind-sight. My expanded point of view neither sanctioned nor defended; rather, it clarified and validated. And that clarification and validation shifted me toward the light, toward understanding and compassion, allowing me to inch forward.

"At that time, in that culture" does not excuse the absurd or rationalize the unacceptable, but it does allow me to see the humanity of the man behind the behavior, a man who did his best with what he knew. And except for the psychopaths of the world, don't we all and haven't we always?

The mother who had her kid's feet x-rayed in the shoe store to insure a good fit, the grandmother who cradled the baby in her arms in the passenger seat, the parents who told their sons and daughters they weren't smart enough, good enough, fill-in-the-blank enough to make them stronger, more resilient to life's vagaries, were acting out of concern and love.

The doctor who prescribed a stiff cocktail for an overwhelmed mother, the experts who advised parents not to talk about the loss of a child, not to bring it up, to just move on with their lives, the priests who counseled women to stay in abusive marriages – all believed they were operating in everyone's best interests.

Mistakes made in the name of progress, in the name of honor, in the name of God, in the name of love.

Wearing my "at that time, in that culture" spectacles, I see that before one is assigned the title of parent, one is a human being with often too little time, too many demands, too much responsibility, and too few resources. I celebrate, through story-telling, the hilarious parts of my experience, and I document the painful to weaken its hold.

Most importantly, I no longer evaluate yesterday's mistakes under today's microscope.

I am committed to not repeating errors, to speaking out when my gut tells me my voice is important. And if I miss such an opportunity, I pray my children know I did the best I could and extract every last bit of humor from my less than perfect parenting.

I hope they look back to the past to understand and appreciate, but not get stuck staring. I pray they have the moxie to paint their own pictures and the courage to include a self-portrait.

And finally I trust they will take responsibility for their lives and understand that, after all is said and done, they are the curators of their own collections.

BE AFRAID, BE VERY AFRAID

When I'm about to take a risk, I consider the downside.
If it's not death, I do it.

~ Nancy Saradella ~

FROM THE FRYING PAN
TO THE FIRE

Ellie Searl

I went to school early to become familiar with the layout of the building and to put my lesson plans and activities in order. The classroom looked like those in the states: rows of flip-top desks with attached swivel chairs; counters strewn with spiral notebooks, teacher's manuals, and paint tins; hanging cupboards stacked with yellowed bank boxes; bulletin boards covered with faded construction paper; dusty green chalk boards; and a stopped-up sink. It even smelled the same - odors of sour milk, musty gym shoes, and bologna hovered in the stale air, trapped by painted-shut, screenless windows.

The school was built for function, not comfort - a series of administrative offices, classrooms along a bleak hallway, open-stalled bathrooms, and a windowless multi-purpose room in the basement, which served as a gym, auditorium, and lunchroom - an adequate facility to hold children captive while they learned the basics of reading, writing, and arithmetic. It didn't matter if kids were hot, cold, bored, or constipated.

I placed a red welcome sign on the bulletin board and a curly ivy on my desk to brighten up the institutional appearance.

It was the middle of October in Quebec. I had been hired to take over a third grade class at Hampstead Elementary School, one of several English-speaking schools of the Protestant School Board of Greater Montreal. According to Carol Miller, the principal, the teacher up and left at recess one day and never returned. A cardinal rule in education is never, but never, leave school children unsupervised. I figured there must have been some nasty mosquito up her butt to cause her to make such a drastic, unprofessional move. Carol thought the teacher had suffered a nervous breakdown. I'll say. I pitied that poor, inexperienced rookie who couldn't manage eight and nine-year olds, not to mention her chosen career.

Educationalese comes in handy during an interview, and I inserted as many phrases as I could without sounding pretentious: Differentiated Instruction, Criterion-referenced Assessments, and all the levels of Bloom's Taxonomy. I was glib and confident. But Carol seemed more interested in my experience as a disciplinarian than in my ability to spout off instructional jargon. It wasn't so much that I had been an elementary teacher for four years in Delaware and Vermont - it was that I had served as a reform school childcare worker in a locked institution for delinquent girls and was currently a group home parent for seven incorrigible female wards of the state who thought all adults were useless.

Carol told me a little about this particular batch of third graders. "They're not quite, ah, how should I put it, obedient. They like to fool around, talk, act silly. They don't pay very close attention to the teacher. They're . . . ah . . . a bit difficult."

If "well, duh," had been a popular phrase at the time, it would have leaked out. What did she expect? These were little kids. Don't little kids fool around? talk? act silly? not pay attention? She thought that was difficult? I wanted the job, and I didn't want to sound impertinent, so I said something diplomatic and professionally strategic. "That's unfortunate. Sounds like they need some rules and a bit of structure."

I knew plenty about bad behavior. I'd had clothes thrown in my face and plastic forks poked into my ribs. I'd been threatened with bread knives and locked in the cellar. Her description of "difficult" sounded like petty annoyances compared to the all but near-death confrontations I'd experienced with crazed adolescent girls bent on making me go berserk.

Carol mentioned something about my having the grit and fortitude to take over this class mid-term without her needing to monitor me very much. She hired me on the spot. I was thrilled. I could switch my housemother's job from full to part time, and my husband, now finished with his McGill class work, could become the full-time housefather. If this teaching gig worked out, we could leave the house parenting business altogether. The sooner I got away from the debilitating turmoil of the group home and the pervasive fear of retaliation, the better. And I was sure we'd make it because it wasn't likely a bunch of little kids from an upscale community of primarily white-collar workers would get my goat.

I stood at the door to greet my new scholars.

The bell rang. They stampeded down the hallway, smashing into each other to be first at the coat rack. Book bags, back packs, lunch pails, jackets, and gym uniforms were thrown hither and yon on the floor beneath the hooks, which stayed empty of a single coat. Shouts tumbled over each other. "Watch out, you jerk, that's mine!" and "Piss off" and "You stepped on my lunch," and "Na-na-na-na-na-na!" and "She's here!" and "Hey guys! We got a new one!" An unintelligible cacophony of little-girl shrieks and little-boy bellows grew into a discordant symphony as though orchestral instruments were fighting for their space on the planet.

I shushed them to quiet down. I tried to make eye contact and speak directly to a couple of them. They neither looked at me nor listened. I picked up a few coats and put them on the hooks. The kids threw them right back to the floor. Nothing worked. One red-headed, freckled boy shoved me aside as he entered the room . "Move over Stupid; you're in my way." He slithered into a desk labeled Jimmy, and swiveled back and forth in his chair until he was greeted by his friends, at which time they moved to the floor under the bulletin board and whispered and giggled and shot defiant glances in my direction.

At the second bell, the rest of the children charged in from the hallway - some to their seats, but most to the floor - chattering with each other as though summer vacation had just begun. I shut the door so the other teachers couldn't see nor hear what was going on, but I think they already knew, considering they had all shut their doors earlier while my students created chaos in the hall. I did wonder why not one teacher had stepped into my room to welcome me, or even give me a generic greeting, "Welcome to Hampstead. Have a nice day."

So there I was - a trained teacher, a tough disciplinarian, and an expert, I thought, at building rapport with youngsters - responsible for the educational progress of 24 banshees who were running around, tossing spiral notebooks, performing hand stands and summersaults in the corner, tearing down my welcome sign, and dumping the dirt out of my curly ivy.

I was in the middle of a teacher's nightmare and I couldn't wake up. Terror swelled my throat shut and cemented my feet to the floor. Paralyzed by indecision, I watched in disbelief as the students poured paint into the sink, drew nude bodies on the board, complete with breasts and penises, smeared Elmer's Glue across the tops of their desks with their forearms, then blew the glue dry so they could peel it off in long strips and roll it up into balls to throw at each other – and me.

Finally, after what seemed like an hour, but was probably just a few minutes, I fixed my voice an octave below normal and boomed at them with the force of a drill sergeant. "STOP! NOW! RIGHT NOW! And SIDDOWN! They stopped and looked at me, a little astonished, I think. No one moved. "I SAID SIDDOWN! NOW!"

One or two kids sat down. Jimmy didn't, nor did his entourage. I threw Jimmy's bottle of Elmer's Glue into the garbage.

"You can't do that – that's mine." He reached for the bottle.

I stuck my foot into the can and pushed the glue toward the bottom, hoping it wouldn't end up on my shoe when I pulled it out. I said, "You touch that glue, and you'll sit in this room with me until midnight!"

"You can't do that either. That's against the law."

"Try me, you little squirt! I'm new here. What do I care?"

Jimmy sat down. Without his glue. But he grinned at me. Then the others sat down, grinning, waiting.

Immediately, my moral code sent me into a tailspin of regret and worry. Each of these evil brats - probably all tattletales - had heard me call Jimmy a nasty name and tell him I didn't care if I broke the law. I needed to recapture my integrity as a teacher and start at the beginning, as if these were normal children in a normal classroom. I introduced myself and wrote my name on the board. "Hi, I'm Mrs. Searl, and I will be your teacher for the rest of the year."

Giggles, taunts, ridicule, hoots, jeers, and heckles. From various desks came new names for me and their echoes. "Mrs. Cereal, Mrs. Serious, Mrs. Hurl, Mrs. Whirl, Twirly Pants, and Mrs. Surly." Other than thinking there must be a smart one in the crowd, I was at once appalled and terrified by the absolute disdain for authority these children were willing to display. The pride they demonstrated for each new corruption of common decency indicated that I needed to watch my back. Nothing, not one thing, in my repertoire of disciplinary techniques worked. I couldn't stop them. I couldn't reason with them. I couldn't control them. They were the most unresponsive beings I had ever encountered, and I was totally out of my element. This group of hell raisers had me in a stranglehold and they knew it. Even the knife-waving, fork-prodding, cellar-door shutting group home girls didn't throw me into as much of a fear cyclone as these little human horrors.

I tried my best to tamp down my panic and ignore the paper airplanes, unauthorized bathroom visits, encores of Elmer's Glue desk-smearing, continued interruptions and manglings of my name, whispering, note passing, farts, burps, and chair swiveling as I struggled to teach one spelling lesson and one math lesson. Only a handful of kids wrote anything on their papers or into their workbooks. The others didn't even bother to take them out of their desks. I figured four out of twenty-four was better than nothing. I could report 1/6 of my school population was responsive. That's good in some cultures.

The lunch bell rang and the kids hightailed it out the door. I heard Jimmy say as he shot by, "Let's see how long it takes to get rid of Mrs. Searl." At least he got the name right.

I recalled the principal's portrayal of this bunch of deranged Dennis the Menaces, these Cujos in human form. "Not obedient. Like to fool around. Talk. Act silly. Won't pay attention. Difficult." Where had my perceptive brain been? I knew how to read between the lines, and I knew how to read people. What had I missed? I must have been so infatuated with the idea of escaping the confines of the group home, I had surrendered my intuitive abilities and seized this job before making a thorough analysis. Who was I to judge their previous teacher? Now I thought of her as courageous for making it all the way through September and into the middle of October with this herd of feral beasts.

I stayed in my room during lunch and tried to reconnect with my humanity. Exhausted and utterly intimidated by this gang of bandits, I was sure I wouldn't get through the rest of the day. And the disappointment at losing an opportunity to quit the group home made me weep.

Then I got mad. *To hell with 'em.* I thought. *Let'm rot. I'll just read stories for the entire afternoon. If they listen, fine. If they don't, fine. I won't be back tomorrow anyway, so it doesn't matter.*

When the students plowed into their seats after lunch, I started to read to them in a very quiet voice. All eyes settled on me. All ears receptive. It was a miracle. I read to them for the rest of the day. As long as I read to them, no one shouted obscenities, no one left for the bathroom, no one mangled my name, and no one squirted glue. A glimmer of civility trickled through. Once the stories were over, all hell broke loose, and we were back to chaos until it was time to go home.

Sheer determination and an ounce of hope sent me back into the ring. I refused to let the fear of Terrible Tiny Town keep me from knocking some decency into their ill-mannered noggins. Very early the next morning, I returned to the classroom with empty boxes and baskets. I removed all items from the students' desks, packed and labeled everything, and stored them on the shelves made by the hanging cupboards around the perimeter of the room.

As the students arrived, I handed each a pencil and a stapled collection of simple math and vocabulary papers. I said, "Sit Down. Do This Work. Don't Talk. When you finish a page, do the next one, and the next one - until you finish the whole thing." The packet had enough work to keep a college sophomore busy. Bored, but busy.

Then I warned them. "If you speak without permission, your name goes on the board. That means five minutes after school. If you speak again without permission, a check goes next to your name. That means another five minutes after school. And each check after that is another five minutes, and so on until you quit speaking without permission. Same thing goes for any type of inappropriate behavior **What. So. Ever**. Got it?" I smiled at them and spoke very softly. "I'll stay all night long. I can stay until tomorrow morning if I have to. See, I brought food - for me. Think I don't mean it? Try me."

When they spoke without permission, I wrote their names on the board. When they whined about doing all that work, I wrote their names on the board. When they complained about their stuff jammed between the ceiling and the cupboards, I wrote their names on the board. If they spoke a second or a third or a fourth time without permission, and they did, I placed checkmarks next to their names. If they asked why I was writing their names on the board, I wrote their names on the board. All morning. All afternoon.

However, when they worked quietly at their seats, I complimented them about anything I could think of. *"You have the nicest blue eyes."* Or *"I like how you write your name on your paper."* Or *"My you finished that quickly – you must like math!"* And especially to Jimmy – *"Wow! Great job with that vocabulary. You really know your stuff!"*

My new approach to behavior control in that classroom saved my sanity and my career. I should have published the program I created that day, because years later, the same concepts and techniques became well-known in the educational arena as *Assertive Discipline,* and had I published mine before Lee and Marlene Cantor published theirs, I could have made millions.

Rather than going into the details of my new program, I'll just mention that by the end of the day, I had five students staying after school, three until 6:30 pm. I jumped through a series of persuasive hoops to get the parents on my side, especially the single mother of the boy I smacked upside the head because his insolence caused my hand to rise with a will of its own, bringing a sobering sting to his left cheek. Carol Miller was sympathetic, but a bit rattled at the thought of police intervention. If the mother didn't sue me, Carol wouldn't fire me. Fortunately, the mother was as disoriented and spacey as her son was unmanageable. She looked at me with over-medicated eyes and murmured, "Gee, Derek must have made you really mad." Then her gaze veered off into the hinterlands of some dream world as she lost all mental contact with her surroundings.

Time, structure, and plenty of consistency transformed the trouble-making energy of these tykes into potentially courteous beings. And it took plenty of resolve to remember that these little butt heads deserved to be appreciated and respected as much as anyone else. I designed and followed a slow, steady educational path, easing into instruction with lots of discipline sandwiched between lots of compliments. By December, they were a functioning class with a modicum of appropriate behaviors and the ability to sit almost through an entire lesson without interruption.

It was at our class Christmas play that I received some recognition for my endeavors. A school psychologist had come to watch Sarah, a particularly needy student, perform the starring role. The play parts had been drawn from a hat, and scrawny Sarah, a skinny kid with decaying, buck teeth, drew the part of Santa. A co-worker told me that Sarah was the worst possible choice for Santa, just as she had told me, on and off since I had arrived, that using worksheets was the worst possible way to educate, regardless of the reason, and keeping kids after school for two hours listening to them vent about their home lives was the worst possible way to discipline, and reading and illustrating stories all afternoon was the worst possible way to teach literature.

The play was a smash hit, and Sarah took her Santa bow with the widest, most rotten-toothed grin ever seen on that stage to the loudest, most appreciative applause ever heard by that class.

Later at lunch, I understand, my skeptic co-worker asked the psychologist what she thought of my teaching style. The psychologist took a sip of her tea, put down the cup, and smiled. "How do you improve perfection?"

That afternoon Jimmy took his book bag and coat off his hook and waved a friendly good-bye. "I liked our play. See you tomorrow, Mrs. Searl."

I may have started in October, but I arrived in December.

NOT EVERY WOMAN'S DREAM

Mary Lou Edwards

Long ago there lived a girl named Thumbelisa who did not want to be a bride. Actually, it was not being a bride that bothered her, it was marriage, but she lived at a time when most maidens became brides, when it was very important to be married.

Thumbelisa had studied ancient civilizations and was not impressed with the Greeks who believed *it a woman's duty to remain indoors and be obedient to her husband* nor with the Romans who declared *a woman had no rights. In law she remained forever a child.* Then there was the Jewish law that said *a wife was owned by her husband.* Even when she dismissed these notions as relics of the past and set aside the biblical teachings that a *wife was to submit to a husband . . . he will dominate you . . . you are subject to him,* she was still looking at wives in the village who were overworked, underappreciated, overwhelmed and undervalued. She was not cut out for matrimony.

Her culture, however, dictated three choices - nun, spinster, wife. Exist under God's thumb, suffer under the King's thumb or languish under the Master's thumb. She couldn't fathom perishing in a convent, much less subsisting as an old maid in the kingdom living with her parents forever. Only saying, "I do," was left. But, adding insult to injury, Thumbelisa had not even a poor prospect, let alone a worthwhile catch. "Settling" was out of the question. Bad enough to shoot her future from a cannon without tethering it to someone she'd *settled for* 'til death do us part.

She'd had a bit of a reprieve because the King believed every maiden should be educated - an unusual notion in the old kingdom. His theory was a maiden needed an education *to fall back on in case she married a louse,* not the most sterling of reasons to pursue learning, but she was not one to stand on ceremony. University bought her time. Her family had always said, "Oh, she's into books, not boys . . ." as though she had to choose between knowledge and knuckleheads. Now, though, her education was complete, and her name was on the marriage roster.

Thumbelisa considered running away, but leaving the village was treasonous. She prayed to St. Quirinus, Patron Saint of Obsessions, since that was what her problem had become. In a state of rapture, a vision appeared and spoke. "It is not the thought of sharing thy life that that thou fearest - it is the thought of having a husband! Get married," the voice commanded, "and pretendeth thou are not. Catholics believeth in denial."

Thumbelisa thought the solution peculiar. She should marry and pretend she was not? Were there knights who would not be tyrants?

She switched her allegiance to St. Raphael, Patron Saint of Friendships and Good Marriages. He would find her a reasonable man - a friend who might then become her partner, her husband.

This was no small order, so she enlisted St. Jude, Patron Saint of Hopeless Causes, too. And before she'd even finished her Nine-Day Never Fail Fast, a prospect appeared.

A man whose values aligned with hers like tumblers in a lock giving access to a space that was safe and comforting.   A friend who allowed her to be herself, who prized an independent woman, who wanted an equal partner.   That - he was an impressive gentleman - handsome, tall and distinguished - was a bonus.   Best of all, he had a great sense of humor - her knight without the armor.

She began to consider taking that leap of faith.

She'd been raised by King Perfect, and that was a harrowing journey, but this knight was better than perfect - he was perfect for her.

From the outside, they were almost a comic study in opposites: tall/short, blonde/brunette, WASP/ethnic, agnostic/Catholic, reserved/brash.   Yet though they differed in background, politics, personalities and demeanor, their hearts were of the same mold.   Neither entertained the notion of changing the other, in part because they were smart enough to know that would be futile, and more importantly, because they loved and accepted the other just the way they were.

"If we wed," she cautioned, "I must keep my coin purse, have my own coach, and journey outside the castle.   I must also maintain my friendships with my maids."

That's up to thee, if that is what thou desires, he would respond, wondering how the seed of dread had been planted.

"Also," she would persist, "we must vow to love, honor, and *respect*, instead of *obey*."

"It is called wedlock," he said, "but you will not be imprisoned."   She had found the perfect traveling companion.

Critical details remained.   It was customary to have long engagements - less than a year raised eyebrows, but if she couldn't get past the betrothal quickly, she would never make it down the aisle.   However, another hurdle remained - the King's imprimatur.

"Are you sure you know what you're doing?" the King inquired, when the Knight asked for Thumbelisa's hand in marriage.   "She is an awful lot of trouble, very strong willed - almost impossible to control, challenges my orders," he ranted. "You will have your hands full. Are you up to the task?"

Those comments gave the Knight a clue as to why her dread was so deep - how a long waiting period might provoke anxiety, cause her to doubt her choice, allow her fears to implode.

Fortunately, while the King was vexed at the suddenness of the wedding, he appreciated divesting himself of the thorn in his side.

They would wed the following month. The event would be put together in record time with just enough trappings to keep the villagers' tongues from wagging. There would be no engagement ring, a borrowed wedding gown, no bridesmaids, simple gold bands, a banquet small by kingdom standards. They would omit the word "obey."

The eve preceding the nuptials, though, King Perfect, who was not happy with the plans, ordered Thumbelisa to tell the Knight to get rid of his beard for the ceremony. "I would prefer a clean-shaven face," he declared.

"He is perfect just the way he is," she smiled.

The morning after as church bells clanged, Thumbelisa handed over her heart.

THE END

FREEFALL

Carolyn B Healy

I was the only kid in Chicago who had never been to Riverview. It wasn't for lack of interest, as I'd been to Kiddieland over and over and was a real fan. It was a matter of logistics. In that era before expressways, when we'd set out for the occasional visit to the relatives in Oak Park, it took forever. And forever in a 1949 Ford, with no air conditioning of course, was no picnic. And Riverview was all the way on the North Side. For all I knew that would take more than forever.

Finally, early in high school came my big chance. My best friend Leslie and I got to go. I remember that. Whether it was it a school trip, or a YMCA outing, or somebody's brave mom who drove us there and then disappeared for a few hours I can't tell you.

We entered the gate and trailed from ride to ride, from The Bobs to Aladdin's Castle, doing whatever we wanted. I felt liberated, grown up, finally part of the larger world. It was delicious.

My traumatic memory begins in the line for the parachute ride, Pair-o-Chutes. Sticky from cotton candy, head spinning from the rides and the lack of supervision, I looked up. Far, far above me loomed the top of the giant tower with two billowing parachutes flapping in the wind. A metal cage dangled and swung from side to side. It was filled with children. They were probably wide-eyed but they were way too far away for me to see.

The machinery clanged, the cage fell and the parachute filled with air. I couldn't see those children's eyes, but suddenly I sure could hear their voices – their terrified screams pierced my ears and opened my brain to the fact that I was waiting in line to do the very same thing. What was I doing here?

You could not call me a brave child, but I had been trying to change that. Every day of elementary school I'd had to pass a yard ruled by a giant gray and black barking dog, one of those muscular mountain types, who would growl at me over the fence. Luckily, the fence was made of just as giant boulders and I believed that he probably couldn't get to me. In eighth grade, I decided that things had to change. Instead of cowering in fear and scurrying by, I would stride by, head held high and show that beast that I wasn't scared of him. Not at all. At the same time I felt that the owners should be ashamed of themselves, terrorizing young children just trying to get to school.

Also, even though I was beside myself with panic whenever I had to go to the dentist, I kept quiet and worked on developing a steely determination to get through it with dignity. Thank God it was only twice a year. If I had a cavity and had to come back sooner, I was wracked with guilt, shame and self-recrimination over this dental failure, not to mention beset by the familiar panic. But I made it through every time and forgot about dentistry until about a week before the next checkup.

So here I was – at Riverview, in line, marching toward certain death, feeling just terrible that my mother would have to face life without me. In my final moments, how would I handle this situation, given my commitment not to chicken out of things? I would have to be brave. I could do it.

On the other hand, how had I let this happen? Part of keeping yourself safe is preventing unnecessary danger, and I'd walked right into this one. My fear told me that this is the kind of thing other people can do but you can't.

In fact, other people even want to do this. I eyed Leslie to look for signs of weakness. She looked up too at the screaming children. And laughed. She would be no help. And since I couldn't bear to out myself as a coward in front of her, no one else could help me either. The line inched forward and carried me slowly to my fate. I remember laboring to keep up lighthearted chatter while my heart was beating wildly out of my chest like in a cartoon.

Maybe I'd be struck with a sudden illness. Maybe I could excuse myself to go to the bathroom and dawdle my way back and, oh well, miss the whole thing. But Leslie was too good a friend. She would loyally step out of line and wait for me. Doggone her anyway.

Or maybe there'd be a power outage, a lightning strike, or . . . or . . . . I ran out of ideas. It was going to happen. We reached the front of the line. The apparatus stopped and the gate flew open. The last occupants, faces glowing with excitement from their fall, were unstrapped and ran toward the exit stairs chattering excitedly.

We climbed in the soon-to-be-dangling basket and were secured in our seats by the bored attendant, who gave the signal with a big wave. We started up.

My terror suddenly broke apart. It was still there, but so was the entrancing and unfamiliar view, the shrinking waves from the crowd below, the silence broken only by the grinding gears. There was a bird. And white clouds against the bluest sky. And the tower, which seemed to still be standing.

I looked up to watch our progress. We were almost to the top. Leslie wasn't saying much either. Maybe she was just a little scared? I couldn't ask.

We hit the top and the terror kicked in full force. The bottom dropped out and we were in freefall, hurtling toward the sidewalk. What if we didn't stop?

But we did. The parachute filled with air, the gears caught, and I was . . . disappointed? At the end, it was not so scary, like going down in an open-air elevator. We hit bottom and clanged into place. It was over. I had lived. Despite the anticlimactic end, I nearly melted into a puddle once my feet hit blessed earth.

The rewards were rich. My thrill came not from the adrenaline rush while falling, but from the post-landing reconfiguration of my identity. I was a person who could do a thing like that after all. I could be terrified, cope with it, and live. I was a survivor. I was brave even. My fear was present and I overcame it. Again. How about that?

But then came the real kicker. It soon hit me that, to be the person I wanted to be, I would need to do this again and again. In the years since I have reenacted my parachute ride repeatedly. Each time, from parasailing off the Florida coast, to the times I've stuck my neck out professionally, to the day my three-year-old had heart surgery, I have found that the measure of my initial fear and dread is about equivalent to the pride and relief after completion.

Good thing I got to Riverview that day. It closed soon after and I might have been left to cower and avoid my way through life. I might have learned this lesson in another way, who knows, but certainly not so quickly or so well. What you learn in freefall sticks with you like nothing else.

RIDING THE WAVES

Some experiences will be sweet, some bitter,
but it's all fine - part and parcel of life.

~ B J Gallagher ~

TRAPPED BY CIRCUMSTANCE

Mary Lou Edwards

"I don't need a University of Wisconsin directory. I need a talented young lady like you to work for me," the man on the other end of the line phone flirted.

Pushing the most recent edition of the UW Alumni Directory, dialing telephone numbers non-stop - busy signals, hang ups, rude refusals - made this alum's response both intriguing and enticing.

Quickly perusing the bio of my potential savior, I noted I was talking to the owner of a well-known photography studio with an impressive Michigan Avenue address.

"Sir," I responded, "I've had my offer of this directory refused, but I have never had such a creative rejection."

"Rejection? Young lady, you come see me tomorrow, and you're hired!" he boomed. I had no idea what his job offer entailed, but escaping the hellhole of tele-marketing was too tempting.

"I will be at your office tomorrow right after work."

"See you then."

From sweatshop to Magnificent Mile in one five-minute phone call? Maybe this would be the Chicago version of Lana Turner's Hollywood discovery at Schwab's Drug Store. I prayed I was worthy of the opportunity. I was the luckiest girl in the world.

The next afternoon I rushed up Michigan Avenue to Valhalla dreaming of working for this prestigious operation. With a bit of luck, I might be able to continue on a part-time basis when I started college in the Fall.

As I ran up the street, I thought of the time I had served at Rockwell Publishing with a hundred quasi-literate dialers, working on commission, elbow to elbow in a boiler room dive hawking this incredibly detailed piece of drek. Even on a good day, it was impossible to make a living wage, never mind college tuition. Hour after hour we dialed Wisconsin graduates with a canned pitch designed to appeal to memories of their glory days. The spiel was lame, but it was worth listening to if only to hear our preposterous rebuttals when an alum was reluctant to waste his money.

If, for instance, someone said he couldn't afford the directory because his house burned down, and he was destitute plus he just found out his wife was the arsonist who wanted him incinerated to collect on his insurance so she could run off with his best friend, I would have a perfect response. Even if he added he was contemplating suicide.

"Sir, now more than ever you need this directory. You cannot pass on this incredible resource. It is filled with names of contractors who will rebuild your torched house, stockbrokers who will make you wealthy, criminal attorneys who will put your wife in jail, divorce lawyers, financial planners, insurance agents who will make your spouse wish she'd not acted so precipitously, and psychiatrists who will help you deal with the pain of betrayal by your best friend. And the support team will all be Badgers eager to assist a Badger brother."

If, by then, the alum wasn't begging for a copy of the directory, I'd continue.

"You will also have this handy referral to help you when you begin dating - hundreds of educated women who need not make money in the sleazy way your soon to be ex-wife tried, women who will renew your will to live. Cultured women who share your love for your alma mater bonding with you during Wisconsin football games.

I guarantee you will not regret purchasing the leather-bound edition."

Fortunately most of the alumni didn't have such complicated problems, but I did use some variation of the above on most solicitations. Sterling Catch, who offered me the job, hadn't even heard my dazzling sales pitch. What impressed him so that he wanted to hire me sight unseen? Was it my precise diction? My sophisticated delivery? Did he detect the conviction in my voice?

It didn't matter. As I hurried along Boul Mich, my focus was on my lucky break.

The Michigan Avenue address reeked of status and respectability. Mr. Catch awaited my arrival and, after a cursory interview, said I could start the next day. Having asked nothing about my education and/or experience, I figured he was just an excellent judge of raw talent. He was, however, a bit vague about my job responsibilities.

"I am designing a position just for you. While I work out the details, you can familiarize yourself with the studio and staff."

A job. created. specifically. for me? I was awestruck.

For the first week.

Then I realized Mr. Catch was the anti-Statue of Liberty, welcoming the hungry and tired, as well as the naive and stupid. He preyed on vulnerable souls.

Years before, he had been the photographer of choice for the North Shore's upper crust, but his glory days were behind him. After succumbing to too many glasses of bubbly and a plethora of sweet, young things, he was left only with arrogance and his extraordinary sales skills. If Mother Teresa herself appeared in his studio, he would have considered seducing her. If she failed to recognize her good fortune, he would interpret the rebuff as her loss, and immediately shift into Super Salesman mode to offer her, at a greatly reduced price because of the sheer volume, individual portrait sittings of every forlorn wretch who had ever crossed her path.

Something in his life had gone awry resulting in vanities and character defects so enormous that even an Oprah intervention would have been wasted. His pathetic staff reflected his predatory proclivity.

Mandi was the Anna Nicole look-alike receptionist who had been married and divorced so many times she stopped changing her last name because of all the paperwork. She was late a lot and had many court dates. Her complex child-support and alimony arrangements, she said, required frequent tweaking, but I suspected the chronic tardiness and incessant lawyers' calls had more to do with her nighttime activities.

Mort, the genius retoucher, smoked in the darkroom, and, I reckoned, drank the photo-developing chemicals in there as well. Like a mole, he ventured out of the darkness only occasionally, blurry-eyed and shaky, searching for "… that bastard Sterling!" who routinely demanded he do the impossible.

Theodosia Goodsell was a munchkin widow who suffered ill-health and was particularly vexed by self-diagnosed "neuralgia" which caused her to disappear for days on end. Only gallons of gin soothed her pain. On her good days, that is, the days she showed up in working condition, Mrs. Goodsell's sales skills put even Mr. Catch's to shame. Her job was to call on the recently bereaved to offer them a once in a lifetime opportunity to order an outrageously overpriced oil painting of their newly deceased loved one. Her frequent slugs from her thermos of "cough syrup" while telephoning potential patsies led to more than a few bizarre scenarios.

Irene, the resident artist was responsible for making the bereaved's dream a reality. She spoke five languages fluently, but only enough English to keep us confused. Her salad days were spent fleeing the Nazis and now, because she'd lost everything in the war, including her academic credentials, she was reduced to painting over huge enlargements of snapshots. Often the head of the subject in the original photo was pea-size and Mr. Catch would insist Mort blow it up to 16x20, thereby obliterating the facial features. It was Irene's job to paint a face that would be somewhat recognizable to the widow. Much of the time, not because of Irene's lack of expertise, the finished portrait resembled a paint-by-number masterpiece.

Completing the off the wall cast was Evelyn Bates, a society woman who'd fallen on hard times. She never quite came to grips with the fact that life had relegated her to soliciting portrait sales from survivors of the dead. She took great pains to maintain the pretense of working "just to keep busy..." but her hopelessly outdated wardrobe, and tales of forty-years past soirees, signaled her denial.

It was an unusual group, but even more peculiar was the fact that there was no photographer on staff. Instead we had a series of photographers who would apply for the "vacancy," work like demons during their unpaid month-long "audition" photographing weddings, bar mitzvahs and debutante debuts and pray they'd get hired. They would cover a variety of events so Mr. Catch could get a "valid sample of your work," but, alas, at the end of a month they never quite had what it took. "You are a competent photographer, but you're missing that 'certain something' I can't explain," Mr. Catch would say. "You're just not a good fit for my North Shore clientele." It was a brilliant never-fail scam.

The Cabinet of Dr. Caligari had nothing on us - a wacko single mother, a talented addict, an ancient alcoholic widow, a Displaced Person who had lost everything in the war, a delusional has-been with a dying husband, an "auditioning" photographer, and a broke college kid.

Trapped by circumstance, desperate for work, we were a captive crew ripe for exploitation. In the days when Polaroid cameras were state-of-the-art, when certain socio-economic groups cherished a snapshot of a loved one the way blue-bloods revered a John Singer Sargent portrait, Mr. Catch carved a predatory niche, and he never looked back.

PADDLING TOWARD TODAY

Carolyn B Healy

I know two people who have been on the Today Show, for very different reasons. The first is Wendy Goldman Rohm, a Chicago area writer and teacher who wrote books on Bill Gates and on Rupert Murdoch, and rode her book tour right in there to appear with Katie and Matt.

A book tour sounds glamorous to someone like me who has never been on one. I imagine I'd love the attention and all the stimulating questions, but Wendy says a book tour is a pain. Apparently answering the same questions all day for weeks gets a little grating. On the plus side, they can never take the Today Show away from her.

On a trip to New York several years ago I spent an hour on the plaza at Rockefeller Center watching the show unfold. I watched Katie, Matt and Al out on the plaza chatting. I could look right through the window and see right where the couch is where the interviews take place. I can just picture Wendy - or me - there. This knowledge has proved most useful in my subsequent viewing.

Celebrities must count on that couch, the makeup, the bright lights to make them look their best. They always look so pleased to be perched there awaiting their segment. Last year I saw a real Today Show celebrity shocker however. All morning they had been teasing an upcoming interview with Kevin Spacey, and when they came back from commercial, there he was on the plaza with them out in the elements, as if he was a visiting weatherman. Kevin Spacey is a Big Star and should have been on that couch. He seemed to agree and made a sad crack about being kept outside. I bet he won't be back at Today very soon.

My second Today Show personality, Emily Kohl, would curl the hair of any parent, which is probably why her story made such a splash. She would remember me only as a basketball mom. I remember her as the scrappy little guard who year after year watched every other girl grow taller and then taller yet. In response, she grew scrappier and scrappier. And that would be where my awareness of Emily would end if not for one post-college venture.

Two years out of college, six years after she had last seen Emily, my daughter received an email. Emily was raising money so that she and a friend could buy a rowboat to take them across the Atlantic Ocean. This is a super fortified industrial strength rowboat that costs upwards of $50,000 if I remember right, a bit over the budget of a couple of post-college young women.

It turns out that there are enough people driven to cross the Atlantic in a rowboat to fill up an entire race, complete with radar, communications equipment and people on shore to monitor progress. Remember when we used to fear that we were raising little girls to be timid weaklings? Cross that one off the list.

They raised the money, launched the boat, and were making decent time 46 days into the race when they were swamped by a 20 foot rogue wave. The boat turned over, water rose inside the cabin and Emily's foot got entangled. She managed to free herself and pull out two life jackets and a sleeping bag. Despite all their grit and confidence, they couldn't right it and had to withstand the elements and hold on for dear life.

That's when the people on shore proved their mettle, summoning a nearby ship filled with young students in a classroom-at-sea project who sped over and picked them up - seventeen hours later.

The fact that these plucky young women had drifted all night, perched on their upside down boat in 10 foot swells and 30 knot winds, wondering when (or if) help would arrive appealed to the morning news cycle. The fact that the rescue ship shot video of their predicament and their relief at being rescued didn't hurt. There was even a subplot: What did the family go through waiting for news? As a matter of luck or grace, Emily's parents had been traveling and heard nothing of her peril until it was over.

So there was Emily and her rescue on the Today Show while Katie Couric, a mother herself, shook her head in alarm. Some days later, when they could make it to New York, both girls sat on that couch, getting far more attention than Kevin Spacey.

In case you breathed a sigh of relief as I did and figured that such a bullet-dodger of an experience would be a once in a lifetime thing, I need to tell you that a couple of years later they did it again and completed the race without a hitch, for which they received much less notice.

I get a boost from Emily's story, something about embracing the thrill of riding the waves instead of huddling in fear on the shore like the rest of us. If I hear that she is trying it again, I'll probably send another check, shake my head and hope that it comes out okay, and that her parents have another trip they can go on. And hope that my own daughter sticks with kayaking.

Beebe Hall

THE DUNKING POOL

Ellie Searl

Love, sex, and religion were not discussed in my household when I was a kid. Each brought embarrassment, awkward stammering, and red faces. Kissing relatives or saying "I love you" was out of the question. My mother once said, "Nobody in my family ever talked about love." Well, neither did she until she got old and we forced it on her.

And sex? That was just a distinction between male and female. When I was sixteen, my mom and I had our one-and-only sex talk. She squinched her forehead, "You know, don't you?" I said, "Yes," and left the room.

It was the same with religion. No questions. No answers. No discussion. Church was just something I did once a week unless I had junior choir rehearsal or youth group later on in high school. The whole system was a big interference in my life. I had better things to do.

If my parents wanted me to believe in a traditional religious doctrine, other than a fundamental, all-encompassing fear of the Almighty, somebody missed the boat. My Federated Church experiences as a kid left me melancholy on Sundays, guilt-ridden all the time, and scared of God. The only thing I liked about church was Communion Sunday when everybody received fresh bread chunks and tiny glasses of Concord grape juice served in silver trays. Other than that, church was a place I endured if I wanted to see the light of day for the next 24 hours.

Westport is on the eastern edge of the Adirondack Mountains where Lake Champlain meanders from Quebec to Lake George, and the western heavens send Canadian Highs directly to our village. We called these glorious visits Westport Days. And if on Sunday the bright rays of a Westport Day stretched across my bed, inviting me to play in the back yard, the thought of spending the best hours of the morning in the dungeons of church made me miserable. I'd curl into a ball and moan and moan until my mother heard the commotion.

It was always the same. Mom lowered the shades and stood over me - hands on hips, fingers tapping the lace of her apron. "If you're too sick to go to church, you're too sick to go anywhere - until tomorrow. That means breakfast, lunch, and supper - right here."

I went to church.

But it wasn't just church – it was Sunday school first and then church. In Sunday school, I sang songs from old hymnals that smelled like my cellar, and I colored pictures of Jesus feeding loaves and fishes from his little lunch bucket to hordes of people at the beach. Our lessons about miracles and creation left me bewildered. It all sounded too preposterous. How could a man, any man, even a great man, walk on water or bring sight to the blind, unless of course, the water was frozen or the eyes had an infection easily cured? And it seemed impossible that God built the earth, animals, and people all by himself. I couldn't even make a decent blueberry muffin for Girl Scouts without help.

Sunday school, church bazaars, spaghetti dinners, choir rehearsals, and the Dreaded Dunkings were held in Beebe Hall, the little white clapboard Baptist church across the street and up the block from the big stone Methodist Church, where the real services were held. We were Federated - merged - because there weren't enough Baptists or Methodists in our town of 800 to keep separate Protestant churches going, especially with the Catholics taking about half the population.

The chapel of Beebe Hall had long wooden pews with musty, threadbare, red velvet cushions and a pump organ with missing keys. Dead center of the altar behind the pulpit, covered by a trap door and a carpet, was a miniature swimming pool, not even long enough for a hamster to get in a good lap. That was where the minister dunked us to purify our souls. The adults called it immersion. I called it terrifying.

I was dunked at thirteen and became – well – Federated, I guess. I went to special classes to learn what to say and do when I was dunked. I don't remember any precepts I memorized before taking this leap into God's territory, and I don't remember any promises I probably made to Jesus or Mary or anyone else on their staff. What I do remember is the terror I felt. First Reverend McDermott would recite a bunch of religious stuff - to which I'd have to agree – and then he'd throw me into the pool. My take on the whole thing was first God would watch me flat-out lie to him, and then I would drown.

God saw everything. He saw me cheat at school and play sick on Sundays. So far, he hadn't hurled any wrath on me, but what would he do once I swore absolute devotion to something I didn't understand and didn't' believe - right in front of my parents, relatives, everybody who came to behold this miracle of salvation, and him? Right under his very own roof? It was fear to the core of my being. Though sometime later I was relieved to learn that Beebe Hall was just a social gathering place, and according to the townspeople, the Baptists hadn't laid any particular claim that their ramshackle bungalow with a steeple was a legitimate House of God.

I stood chest deep in the cold water wearing an adult-sized black choir robe over my favorite blue organdy. I was supposed to take the dress off, but I refused to strip down to my underwear and slip in front of anybody. My Sunday school teacher tried to get me to undress in the bathroom or coat closet, but I wouldn't do that either. If I was supposed to take my clothes off, what was the minister wearing? The idea that he might be standing next to me in his underwear horrified me.

So there I was in the dunking pool, pressing air puffs out of my billowing robe, freezing, trembling, and scared, feeling broken tiles and grit on the bottoms of my feet, wondering when Rev. McDermott would shove me into the water and whether or not this withered old man had the strength to lift me up again? There was no rehearsal in dunking.

On cue, I pledged the requisite allegiances to God and testified to my faith – Baptist? Methodist? I didn't know. Then Reverend McDermott put his hands on my back and stomach and plunged me backward into the dunking pool. My flailing arms couldn't find my nose, and I breathed in pool water up to my eyebrows. I rose out of the water sputtering, coughing, spewing water, and shivering – with sopping hair and my water-heavy robe, dress, and underwear clinging to my skin. Everyone clapped and retired to the social hall for cookies and punch to celebrate my rite of passage.

Besieged by humiliation, I ran into the girls' bathroom before anyone could congratulate me and sobbed - and sobbed - about what? Lying to God? Not comprehending this mystery everyone else seemed to grasp? Being drenched and wrecking my favorite dress? Or being thirteen and forced to go through such mortifying hoops to become an adult?

I was the star of the party, but I didn't want well-wishers staring at my sopping head and soaked dress. I refused to come out of the bathroom until my mother brought me dry underwear, another dress, and a barrette to hold back my straggling hair. When I finally joined the guests, I sat in a corner beside the kitchen and stared at the floor, arms crossed, mad at everything, especially church. I didn't speak. My mother thought I was really sick, so she took me home and sent me to bed. It was the one time I went willingly to the isolation of my darkened room in the middle of the day.

For years I waited for God to wield his hammer on me for my hideous behavior and lack of devotion, but he must have figured my goodness as a person and my strong moral code was worth something, because from what I can tell, he never saw the need to make me pay for my transgressions.

Today I look for truth in the natural world. I am far too pragmatic to subscribe to the idea that a supernatural being built the planets and their pathways around the sun. However, the mysteries of the universe baffle me, and the vastness of the cosmos gives me pause. I marvel at the enormity of the heavens and the secrets of nature - Orion, Cassiopeia, and the North Star; Venus peeking over the horizon; the reappearance of birds and buds every spring, and the monarch butterfly's 5,000-mile flight to Mexico.

I accept these heavenly and earthly wonders with a thankful grace. As long as I remain a virtuous person with virtuous intentions, and as long as I tend our world with care, I'm satisfied I've lived up to my part of any bargain I may have made.

MOTHERHOOD

My mother had a great deal of trouble with me,
but I think she enjoyed it.

~ Mark Twain ~

MOTHER OF THE YEAR

Carolyn B Healy

Elizabeth Edwards slogs forward on her book tour, pundits lob shame-bombs at her, and I cultivate a growing resentment about the whole scenario. My friend Kathy and I even had a spat about her the other night. Kathy thinks she should just stop talking and toss her husband to the curb. Kathy thinks she's pathetic. I think she's anything but.

I'd like to talk about Elizabeth without wasting too much time on husband John. Kathy and I agree on him. Let's just stipulate that he's the guy you hope your daughter won't meet. Too good-looking to have been required to develop character, although well-trained in creating and cultivating appearances. An overgrown adolescent. If you don't agree on the last point, watch clips of his coy flirtation with the videographer he took up with. A middle-schooler lusting after the new social studies teacher wouldn't display such leering desire. Narcissistic, arrogant. The good-guy imposter genus of the liar-cheater species of the human male. Yeah, yeah. He's also done good works. He should have stuck with those.

Elizabeth is everywhere these days, promoting her book *Resilience*, and risking media saturation. So are her critics, who dump truckloads of directives at her feet about how she should feel, talk, and act. I'd like a word with those critics.

I'm a therapist, so listening to people in tough spots is nothing new to me. When I hear Elizabeth refuse to use the other woman's name or decline to contemplate the paternity of her child, or express more vitriol for the other woman than for her husband, I don't hear what the critics do - that she is willfully hiding from the truth, deluding herself, letting him off the hook so that she can stay in the spotlight.

Instead, I hear her stating emphatically: I'm at capacity. One more thing and I'll crack.

Of course she's in denial. Any healthy person would be. In fact, I believe fervently in denial. It gets a bad rap in the pop culture rush to erase all negative emotion and usher sufferers into closure, whatever that is. It's portrayed as a thing to get out of. But not so fast. Denial gets us through what is unbearable, as well it should, and it lasts as long as it lasts, until we don't need it anymore.

To me, the popular bromide that God never gives you more than you can handle is a dangerous lie. Tell it to the many clients I have seen swamped by tragedy yet criticized by onlookers for not responding as they would like. We are only human. We need a temporary trauma regulator, a valve that protects us from overload. Denial is that fail-safe device, part of the hard-wired security system that automatically kicks in when we are overrun by life's torments. Take that away from Elizabeth and where is she?

Think of what she has lost. Her son Wade many years ago, and all she hoped his life would include. Her health. The loving marriage she thought she had. Her children's security. Her future. This is about grief and only about grief.

Here's how it works. Each new loss reactivates the ones before, and we drag all of them along with us for a time, until we can begin to reassemble a life that makes sense.

Why does Elizabeth get the rest of us so stirred up? Certainly her honesty about her medical condition unsettles us, and her blind spots about her cheating husband infuriate us. Her choice to stay married to him disappoints us, but we don't get to prescribe how another carries out her grief.

She is living out our worst nightmares, but if we turn on her for the way she is doing it, we do none of us justice. And, speaking of arrogance, to imagine that the rest of us know what we'd do in her awful circumstance is at least naïve, and more likely evidence that we're in denial ourselves.

Here is the elephant in the room that Elizabeth sees and her critics can't: She is going to die and her children will have the shock of their lives – the kind of shock that will change them forever – their brains, their trajectories, security, expectations, worldview. Her death will cost them in a thousand ways. Grief will climb on board and accompany each of them through the rest of their lives.

While the opinion snipers accuse her of complicity, passive-aggressiveness and the rest, Elizabeth stays put, preserving stability for her children, cushioning them from additional upheavals. She knows that they will end up with their father, and is saving them a side trip into divorce and further trauma. She has a higher mission than pleasing her critics. It's not that John is worthy of her loyalty, but her children are.

She is colluding – with the notion that they are a family and that John is the person she entrusts with their future. If she has to turn away from full-reality living for a time to accomplish that, to allow herself to direct her attention to the parts of her life that she can still control, so be it.

Her disease has taken away her chance to see her life unfold the way she'd hoped. So did her son's death. So did her husband's actions. The rest of us shouldn't take away her opportunity to complete the things she can control as she sees fit.

There's one more thing I hear her saying: I may not have much time. But I have something to say, and it wouldn't kill you to listen. I've been places you haven't and know things that you don't.

The rest of us might learn something if we'd settle down and listen to her. We'll know to thank our lucky stars that for most of us, our particular burdens right now pale in comparison to hers. We'll know to hug our kids, smile at our partners, and locate our compassion.

MY MOMMY IS BETTER THAN YOURS

Ellie Searl

I knew my daughter, Katie, would be a far more charitable parent than I when she was twelve. It was while she was babysitting our four-year old neighbor, Laurie, an outspoken, precocious child. You know the type. The over-indulged genius-spawns who are taught that adult conversation is of minimal significance, and interrupting a discussion about mortgage meltdowns or the President meeting with dignitaries in the Middle East with such earth-shattering news as, *Mommy, see? I made the letter L,* is a far more critical issue in the scheme of world events.

Such children are encouraged to speak their minds – no matter what. They'll stare into a poor soul's face and say, *That fat man looks like a gorilla* – when he unfortunately does – and the mother, in her need to take every opportunity to reinforce her child's powers of perception and add yet another word to the child's burgeoning, and annoying, vocabulary, responds with, *Yes, Honey-Bunch, aren't you the observant one! Observant means you see things very accurately,* "accurately" having been taught the day before during dinner while the family contrasted the various green shades of arugula, pesto, and blanched broccoli.

Katie bent down to buckle Laurie's Mary Janes. The little imp held onto Katie's shoulder with her right hand, pointed at me with her left, and announced, in her usual whiny tone, "I don't like you. You're *mean*." Then she put her hand on her hip and said to the top of Katie's head, "I like *my* mommy better than *yours*."

My first impulse was to reproach this insufferable undersized snot with, *Hey, you spoiled brat, that's no way to talk. Don't your parents teach you to be polite? Oh, and polite means nice – as in times you aren't spanked*, when Katie piped up with a soft, "Of course you do. She's your own mommy. Everyone loves his or her own mommy best. I love my mommy best of all, too." Katie looked up at me and smiled as she pushed the leather strap through the buckle. "There, Laurie. You're all set. Let's go for our walk."

That was it. No blame, no recriminations, no scolding. Just appreciation and that esteemed attribute, so necessary in parenting - pure acceptance. Chagrinned, I snapped my jaw shut and reflected on the difference between my at-the-ready disapproving response and Katie's generous one.

Pandering to over-pampered children has never been my forte. Perhaps it's because I taught school for so many years and encountered bunches of coddled kids whose parents thought their children's proverbial shit didn't smell. They say teachers don't have pets. Well, they do - and their pets are those kids who respect the world and the people in it. Actually, truth be told, teachers' pets are those kids whose parents are so aware of their child's stinky shit, they'll tell you themselves.

I remember one seventh-grade boy in particular. Ryan. This kid's sneer suggested he possessed information only the devil could appreciate - and his swagger suggested he was about to act on it. He disrupted class with sniggering, throwing stuff, and just acting like a smart ass most of the time.

The boy was bad enough, but it was his mother who really pissed me off. She worked as a nurse's aide in a nearby middle school, so you'd think she'd be sensitive to the typical shenanigans of twelve-year-olds, and perhaps even be aware of the appalling behaviors of her own son. She wasn't.

One day I was forced to discipline Ryan for blatant insubordination and outright defiance. He was to stay after school for a thirty-minute "meeting" with me to review his disobedient classroom behavior and come up with a plan for improvement.

It was mandatory in my school district to notify, in writing, in advance, the parent of a child who was to serve an after-school detention - no matter what. That meant I had to fill out a Disciplinary Notice of Non-Compliance, documenting everything. Name, grade, advisor, crime committed, location and time of incident, how the behavior was out of compliance with the Code of Conduct, and the disciplinary measures I would take to help improve the child's wayward behaviors.

So I did. I filled out the form and gave it to Ryan after class, telling him that he was to take the form to his mom so she could read and sign it, bring it back in the morning, and then stay after school with me in the afternoon so we could develop his Improvement Plan together.

"I'm not staying after school tomorrow." He grinned. "You wait and see." He grabbed the form and walked off

Early the next day I received a phone call from Ryan's mother. "How dare you try to keep my son after school? Who do you think you are?"

Startled, I took a second to regroup, and then said in my most welcoming voice, "Oh . . . Hi . . . Mrs. Hollister. Thanks for calling. Did you see the disciplinary form I sent home with Ryan yesterday?"

"You're damned right I saw it. I got the damned form right here in front of me. What do you mean by *non-compliant* and *defiant*?"

"Well," I said, "non-compliant means he isn't going along with what is required here at school, and defiant means he isn't obeying the . . ."

"What do you think, I'm an idiot? I know what non-compliant and defiant mean."

"You asked what they meant."

"No, I want to know why you *wrote* non-compliant and defiant on this *God-damned* form! He's only a little kid. He's twelve years old for *Christ sake*."

"He disrupts my class."

"He's an active boy. He enjoys life. You teachers are all alike. You people just want robots in your classrooms."

"He is rude and disrespectful. He shouts out obscenities, he walks around the room during our lessons, he's mean to the other students - he takes their things."

"I don't call that non-compliant. *Or* defiant. That's just energy. And I don't appreciate you writing anything like that on this form here. I'm throwing this away, and you better get rid of yours. It's not going in any file. You're out of line. Oh, and by the way, he's not staying after school."

My heart started to pound. I could feel my emotional state begin to disintegrate. Built-up hostility and rancor toward all those parents who defended the monstrous actions of their terrible children took over my ability to reason. Any good judgment I had stored up became useless - paralyzed. My mouth opened and the awful truth poured out of me as never before in my entire career. I couldn't hold back.

"Mrs. Hollister," I said, "I think you should pay more attention to your son's colossally obnoxious behavior than the wording on a disciplinary form. He's a shit-faced spoiled brat and one of these days someone is going to give him a much needed kick in the rear. You are a coddling mother who thinks her kid's poop doesn't leave stains. And because of your inability to see the oversized layers of crap in your precious juvenile delinquent of a son, he will either end up doing time in the local detention center for youthful criminals or get pitched into a backyard garbage dumpster by an annoyed neighbor before he's old enough to see an R-Rated movie. Oh, and by the way, I will deny ever saying any of this to you."

She may have tried to interrupt me during this harangue, but I kept on in a fury, fueled by years of pent-up adrenaline and bad-will toward inadequate parenting. Then I hung up. A rush of blood flooded my face and burned my ears. I had to remind myself to breathe. It took several minutes to settle into a modicum of my usual teacher mode and attitude, but then, throughout the rest of the morning, I felt strangely calm, as though I had just risen from a deep-tissue, full-body massage.

The principal called me into the office later that day. Mrs. Hollister had a reputation for being an insufferable, over-protective parent, but I had a reputation for being a fair, honest, gracious teacher. Her accusations were of little consequence. "What did she say I said? Really? That's terrible! Imagine." And so on. Poor Mrs. Hollister. No credibility. No resolution.

And Ryan? He still acted like a jerk in my classroom, and I still tried, albeit unsuccessfully, to guide him into becoming a citizen of the world. I figured it was best to steer clear of his mother.

Between Ryan's seventh and eighth grade years, he and his mom moved to Reno, Nevada. They are now probably quite prosperous, grifting their way through small-town America.

DISGUSTING
FOUR-LETTER WORDS

Mary Lou Edwards

My friend, Domenica, maintained that after a woman got married, if she kept a clean house and didn't get fat, she could be an axe murderer and no one would care. Men reserved a particular scorn for wives who did not keep a house spic and span or who, God forbid, "let themselves go," but I feared the scorn of men far less than I feared household drudgery which I suspected caused brain damage.   Polish furniture that was already shining? Scrub floors that weren't even scuffed? Launder clean curtains just because it was Monday? *No way.*

I considered housework a form of domestic violence and C-O-O-K, I-R-O-N, and D-U-S-T offensive four-letter words. My aversion was not genetic. My mother's housekeeping made Polish cleaning ladies look like slackers, and she was a world-class cook on top of it. 'Til today I rarely eat in an Italian restaurant since no dish ever comes even kind of close to hers.

I could claim I was intimidated by her extraordinary culinary skills, but I'd be lying. The truth was preparing, cooking, cleaning up three times a day, for a family that considered memorable meals an inalienable birthright, was just not part of my plan. I was not going to be trapped in a kitchen.

It wasn't as though my mother didn't try to steer me toward domesticity.

"Mary Lou," she'd say as she stirred at the stove, "come watch how I do this."

"Just give me the recipe, Ma."

"Recipe? What recipe? You need to *see* how I make it. Someday you'll be sorry you didn't learn how to do this."

"Ma, I'm going to college. I don't need to know how to cook."

"Don't be crazy. College people eat. What are you going to do when you get married?"

"I probably won't get married and, if I do, I'll find a man who's not that into food. Or I'll marry someone who likes to eat out," I said, thinking of solutions on the spot. "Then again, maybe we'll just eat at your house every night, or my husband will cook like Daddy."

"Cook like your father?" she responded, her eyebrows leaping to the ceiling.

"I saw Daddy make eggs for breakfast once."

"It was probably when Nonna was dying and I was sitting vigil at the hospital."

"Well, it was the only time I ever saw him cook, but you never know. Look at Bo."

My father's friend, Bo, made the best sopresatta in the world. To this day, not here or in Italy, have I ever found anything that could compare. Just the thought of walking past his house and spying the mini-salamis hanging by their strings air-drying in his attic makes me yearn for giardineria with fresh Italian bread.

"I could marry a chef. Ma, did you know women can't be chefs?" I said, trying to take the spotlight off my recalcitrance. "I read that all of the world's great chefs are men."

"Sure," my mother smirked, "when a man cooks they call him a chef and pay him big money. Mothers make great food every day, but they're just plain old cooks."

"But, Mom," I teased, pecking her on the cheek, "you get paid in love."

"I know. I know. I'm a lucky woman," she smiled. "I always wanted to be a wife and mother. I'm not complaining."

You should complain I thought. *If I were you, I'd be complaining big-time*. What is so rewarding about having floors you could eat off of or shining kitchen tile every week with Jubilee?

Perhaps none of this appealed to me because I was a disaster at it. Even when I tried, I got it all wrong.

Once I attempted to help my mother with the ironing, but I had no sooner dug into the bushel basket when she yanked the iron's cord from the wall socket.

"Your father would never wear such wrinkly underwear, and you scorched this pillowcase. You're impossible," she railed, as she collapsed the ironing board with a thud almost amputating my fingers. If I'd known that a burned pillowcase would be my ticket to freedom, I'd have scorched from the get-go.

Mama was right though - I was impossibly incompetent. I couldn't even hang laundry right. I let the sheets drag on the grass because I forgot to use the pole to prop up the clothesline. I hung the socks by the ankle instead of the toes. I mixed articles of clothing instead of grouping them. And my towel hanging was a "complete disgrace."

"Look at how you hang towels," she said with disgust. "You're using two clothespins for every towel and wasting clothesline between them."

"Ma, you make it sound like there's a clothespin shortage."

"Keep it up, Mary Lou, and you're going to be in real trouble. Try following directions, for a change. Put one towel on the line and put a clothespin in the left corner," she demonstrated, "then instead of wasting another clothespin, take the second towel and lap it over the first a tiny bit and use another clothespin to hold the two together, then add another towel and do the same thing and keep going until you've hung all the towels together. For every two towels you should only use three clothespins. I'll watch you finish this row."

"Ma, you have got to be kidding? This is moronic," I argued, "I can't believe you expect me to do this. Let's get wild and crazy, throw in a few extra clothespins, and really live it up."

"*Capo tosto!* You're such a hardhead, you never listen," she scolded. "You think everything's a joke. You're hanging things willy-nilly. Put all the handkerchiefs together, all the dishtowels together." Lowering her voice to a stage whisper, she added, "And hang the underpants on the inside clothesline where the whole world can't see them."

"Mother," I protested, "I think the neighbors *know* we wear underpants and brassieres. I mean, *what's the big secret?*"

"Shame on you - panties are private, hide them on the inside. Put the sheets and towels on the outside lines so the sun can get at them, and quit being a smart-aleck."

I hated the tasks I was given, and I was always deemed too young for the jobs I coveted.

I yearned to wash windows sitting half outside on the windowsill, my legs dangling in the house, my torso outside, my face reflected in the glass, and pull the window sash down on my lap to squeegee. Jenny Next Door used to sit almost totally outside on her third floor sill holding onto the frame with one hand, squirting her vinegar spray bottle with the other. Gawking from my back porch, my Popsicle dripping on my pedal pushers, I was amazed at her courage, mesmerized by her dexterity. Once, and I am not kidding, *she even stood up outside on the sill to reach the upper sash*, one hand holding on, the other swiping the rag back and forth, and all the while she yelled at her sons down in the yard who were chasing each other with a hammer.

"Ma," I begged, "please, if you let me wash windows sitting half outside like Jenny Next Door, I promise I'll make them sparkle."

"No," she said, "you have to be at least fourteen to do that. The last thing I need is to find your body crumpled in the gangway. People would never stop talking and you'd probably leave the windows streaky."

"We live on the first floor, for crying out loud," I whined. You just don't want me to have any fun."

"Knowing you, Sarah Bernhardt, you'll fall out the window and crack your skull just to get attention, and I'll have to sit vigil in the hospital. You can run around on window ledges all you want after you're married, and your husband has to worry about you."

I think she knew, before I knew, that my ineptitude was a subversive form of passive resistance. Somewhere deep inside my little noggin I must have realized that if I excelled at domesticity, I'd be signing my own death warrant. My mother, however, attributed my aversion to a ". . . combination of laziness and reading too many damn books." She refused to accept that the only thing domestic about me was that I was born in this country.

One of her last ditch efforts was registering me for eight weeks of sewing lessons at the Salvation Army Settlement House - commonly known as "The Sal," where mostly non-Catholic urchins ran amok. Perhaps she thought she'd appeal to my creative side but, alas, I continually jammed the sewing machine while trying to fashion her Mother's Day gift of a tea apron. I assured the teacher my mom did not need a tea apron because she only drank coffee, but Mrs. Muscolino snarled, "You are making a tea apron, and your mother will love it!" In the eleventh hour, when I burned out the pedal on the sewing machine, Mrs. M took pity and gave me a needle and thread, but I had no luck with that either so I stapled on the waist ties. I considered glue, but I figured staples would hold up better knowing my mother's propensity for obsessive laundering.

Mrs. M checked over the finished product. "What exactly do you think your mother is going to be putting in this pocket? It could hold a St. Joseph's table full of food. And the waist ties? They're supposed to be *equal* in length." Whipping off her measuring tape from around her neck, she said, "One of the ties is four inches, the-other-is-fourteen. Unless your mother has the waist of a wasp, this will *never* fit her."

"Well, if the ties are too short she can give it to the lady upstairs. Her baby could use it as a bib and keep her toys in the pocket," I suggested, vowing never to sew another blessed thing as long as I lived.

On Mother's Day, after we gobbled up the delicious frittata my mother cooked, my brother, sister and I brought out our presents.

She opened my brother's first.

He gave her a breathtaking Our Lady of Fatima statue. Our Lady was standing on a blue plastic ball, which my brother said was the world. I could see how he thought that, because it was round like the Earth, but, hello, the world is not blue. And besides, it was Jesus who walked on water, Mary walked on land, so it was sort of stupid, I thought.

"It's not the Earth - it's blue like the ocean. There's no *land*," I snapped. Meanwhile, my mother was acting like he gave her a relic from the Vatican. Shooting me a dirty look and completely ignoring my input, my brother played his trump card.

"Ma, twist the globe - it opens." Sure enough, she twisted and this huge black rosary fell out of the ocean. "Anthony," she exclaimed, "I will treasure this forever." He stood there beaming like an altar boy who gets to lead the casket out of the church after a funeral. I felt like snapping Our Lady off her perch, but I was not going to commit a Mortal Sin and risk going to Hell because of my brother. It was always obvious my mother adored him just because he was her first-born and only son. As far as she was concerned he could do no wrong, and she rarely punished him for anything. Once I saw him actually walk into our kitchen with his muddy baseball spikes on, and she barely yelled at him. The truth was if he had given her an elbow macaroni necklace, she'd have been just as over the moon so I pretended I didn't care, but secretly I had to admit it was a very cool present. The way the ocean twisted open around the equator, and the giant rosary beads fell out, was extremely impressive.

My sister gave Mom a floral handkerchief on which she'd embroidered MOTHER. I didn't think it was a big deal but my mother said, "Oh, Anna, this is just what I needed. How did you know?" as though she didn't have an entire drawer full of cleaned and pressed hankies.

"Open mine, open mine, Ma, I sewed it just for you at the Sal," I screeched, remembering Mrs. M's wasp-waist comment. My mother opened the box and pulled out the apron. "Ohhhhh, isn't this *interesting*," she said, as though I'd given her a stupid pencil holder made out of a tuna fish can.

My brother, still smarting from the fact that I had pointed out Our Lady of Fatima was standing on the ocean, and piped up, "Is that supposed to be an apron? It looks like a cockeyed shopping bag, if you ask me. You could fill it up with a million raviolis. Besides, she didn't even sew it - it's a bunch of staples. And you'll have to tie it around your neck."

"No one asked you, Anthony," my mother said, shooting him the evil eye. "I'm sure your sister worked very hard on this."

My father sat at the kitchen table with a "what the hell is that" look on his face (he was into details like measuring and neatness) my mother looked up from the tea apron and said quietly, "Mary Lou, you must stay on the Honor Roll and do well in school. You will never make it as a housewife."

After the apron bust, little was asked of me outside of picking up dog crap in our yard, running errands and drying dishes.

I could see I was a huge disappointment to my mother. I begged for God's help with my domestic disability.

Dear God, please send me a rich husband so we can have a housekeeper. My mother has told You over and over 'God, this girl will never learn to do housework!' and You know she is right. If he's handsome, smart and likes to have fun that would be excellent, but really the maid thing is the most important. There's no hurry, You know I have to go to college first, but please start looking for him now because everyone says it's going to be impossible to find a husband interested in a wife who only wants to read books all day. If you can't find a rich one for me, at least find one who doesn't care about home-cooked food or ironed clothes. AMEN.

I prayed often, and it worked, sort of. God sent me a husband with all my requirements, except he was not rich, and, here is where I knew God was really on the job. My mother-in-law had been such a horrible cook my husband thought Cheerios with a banana was a gourmet dinner. If I so much as made toast, which I didn't do often, he was grateful. Thanks to peanut butter and jelly, lunchmeat, cereal and carry-out, we did just fine. Occasionally I went all out and cooked, but I always seemed to miss the mark.

In a fit of madness one day, I decided to make fried smelts for supper. I have no idea what possessed me, but it sounded easy enough when I overheard someone say you just put oil in a frying pan and throw in the smelts. So I cut off their heads, sickened by their beady little eyes, and dumped them into the hot oil. Had I done this *and* stayed in the kitchen, we might have had a home-cooked meal. Instead, someone called needing a phone number which I went upstairs to retrieve. As I stood on the landing returning to the kitchen, phone number in hand, black smoke billowed up the stairwell. Taking a deep breath, I flew down the stairs and out the front door, sooty and shaking.

Standing across the street from my house, I saw the smoke pouring out the front door, and I knew my husband was going to be furious. Several months earlier, he'd been really aggravated when the microwave door blew off while I was sterilizing my contact lenses, and that little caper had only involved replacing the microwave and patching a hole in the wall. He was going to be over the top if the house burned down. Fortunately, a neighbor called the Fire Department, and the hook and ladder arrived minutes before my husband pulled up and jumped out of his car leaving it in the middle of the street.

At least a dozen firemen charged through the front door, giant boots flapping, pick-axes at the ready, smashing out windows.

"What happened? Where's my wife?" my husband shouted as I came charging across the street to explain.

"Are you OK? What happened?" he hollered amidst the chaos. "Did something explode? Were you smoking? What the hell is going on?" he asked as the flames waved hello out the kitchen window.

Just then the fire chief, in a huge rubber raincoat with Chicago Fire Department emblazoned on the back, walked toward us.

"Don't worry, sir. We've got this under control," he reassured my husband. "It's a run-of-the-mill kitchen fire - lots of smoke, not too much damage. We knocked out some windows and the cabinets are shot, but it looks like we can save the rest of the house." Turning to me, he said, "And you, little woman, better be more careful when you're cooking dinner."

"Cooking dinner?" my husband choked out, his eyes the size of extra large pizzas. *"You were cooking? In the kitchen? At the stove?"*

"Yes," I said. "Yes, I was frying smelts."

"Frying smelts? Like fish smelts?"

"Yes, I wanted to surprise you by frying smelts."

"What in God's name were you thinking? Smelts? We've never had smelts. I cannot believe that you were trying to cook smelts."

I was getting a bit annoyed with his shock and disbelief, acting like I'd never stepped foot in the kitchen. Was he forgetting I worked my fingers to the bone making chicken wings every Super Bowl Sunday? Was he blocking on the fact that one Thanksgiving I cooked a turkey that sent my mother-in-law to the ER? I mean, it wasn't as though I never cooked.

"I wanted to surprise you by frying smelts," I sniveled. "They're not that hard to make."

"Not that hard? They're flinging kitchen chairs out the window. You've practically burned down the freakin' house. Whatever possessed you?"

"I don't know," I said shrugging. "All of a sudden I felt like cooking. *Is that such a sin?*" I wanted to add *you ungrateful bastard* but the neighbors were crowding around, jumping over the fire hoses ostensibly to comfort us, but really to be nosy. "I can't explain what came over me."

A year prior when we were having the kitchen redone, the remodeler was peppering me with questions. "So what kind of fridge do you want? Side by side, freezer at the top, ice-maker on the door? Cold water dispenser? Twenty-four cubic feet?"

"Look," I had told him, "I just want a plain old refrigerator. I'm not really into kitchens. If I had my way, we'd turn this room into a den, but my husband says that would hurt the resale value."
"Yeah," he had said, "most buyers have a kitchen on their wish list."
So we put in the new kitchen, and now it was in shambles.

"Promise me, look into my eyes and promise me you'll never do this again," my husband pleaded as the firemen gave the all-clear sign. "You could have been incinerated."

"OK, alright, I promise," I assured him. "If the smelts had turned out, I was going to bake you a birthday cake next week but now I won't even bother."

"Good. That's why God invented bakeries."

About six months later, in another fit of impulsive recklessness, I decided to make an egg.

"Honey," I yelled, "have you seen my frying pan? I've searched everywhere."

With a look of alarm, he walked into the kitchen. "Yes, I did see the frying pan. Do you remember when you set the house on fire frying smelts?"

His tone of voice suggested I was some kind of demented pyromaniac.

"Well, during the blaze," he continued in a Mr. Roger's voice, "the firemen threw the skillet out the window. When the snow melted in the

Spring, I found the pan and threw it in the garbage. Is this the first time you've noticed it's gone?"

Apparently he'd forgotten he made me promise not to cook so I ignored his snide remark.

"Thanks a lot," I snipped, highly insulted. "You at least could have told me it was trashed. That was a very expensive frying pan I got for my shower and I hardly used it. Now I have to go to the hardware store and buy another one. How am I supposed to bake a cake or fry an egg with no skillet?"

"You're not supposed to - grab your coat," he said. "We're going out for breakfast."

.

IF WE DON'T LAUGH, WE'LL CRY

*You need to claim the events in your life
in order to make yourself yours.*

~ Anne Wilson Schaef ~

JUST A KID

Ellie Searl

He was just a kid, and he used to live in that shack-turned-shrine.

Gaudy bouquets of sagging paper roses fall into weeds. Wrinkled posters scrawled in black magic marker, "Rest in Peace," and "I will love you forever," above a distorted sketch of his face - the ink, purple from rain and dew, bleeds across the page. Candles, balloons, American flags, and melted candy lump together in piles. Stuffed animals - bears and tigers and dogs - with faded bows and grubby, matted fur, are topsy-turvy, tossed among crumpled sympathy cards and hand-written notes.

Slumped mourners take snapshots of each other, marking history and capturing tears of personal loss in front of the twisted, yellow Do Not Cross police barrier, stretching from the fence, around the stubby tree -

jammed with soggy dolls, hand-made gifts, and toys – into the bareness of the backyard.

And across the street, protected from the hot sun and rain by black and white striped tent awnings, card tables are stacked with souvenirs. Over-sized tee shirts, CD's, and DVD's - each on sale for the low, low price of $15.00. "Get your tee shirts here!" Seems like a deal. Mourners pocket their cameras and hold up shirts to their chests. "Do you think I look better in this one? Or this one?" Boom boxes at top volume play "I'll Be There," and "Thriller," and "Billy Jean."

He was just a kid. A cute, black kid. One of nine - all squeezed together in a foursquare shack - all trying to find space, like too many broken crayons shoved into a torn, over-used box.

He was just a kid. Handsome. Talented. Could he sing! And dance!
He was the best of the five. He was the lead. Still, just a kid. And all the while, they say, as he was growing up, they say, he was filled with fear. He cried and endured the onslaughts of an abusive dad, they say.

He and his brothers were very well behaved. Their dad made sure of that. No playtime, no running around the backyard, no friends, not even real school – just rehearse and perform. Rehearse and perform. Entering contests. Winning competitions. Entertaining the patrons of black nightclubs from Chicago to DC. Then Motown. Then LA. Then Neverland. Then . . . what?

He was just a kid who grew from a sweet, round-faced Gary, Indiana, toddler into an exceptional and celebrated entertainer and into stardom and world-wide fame and then into a grotesque, disfigured, emaciated man-child who liked to spread love by sleeping with little boys after serving them the wine he called "Jesus Juice."

That tiny, garage-shaped home - an empty, rotting, paint-chipped, clapboard house - now the backdrop of a massive mound of tributes to the one who had captured the hearts of devoted fans and had filled the pocketbooks of enabling promoters and had satisfied the photo-lust of the paparazzi and had crammed the agenda of the media and then, after years of mystery, and innuendo, and hanging his baby over a balcony, and being tried for pedophilia, and reshaping his body into a sculpture so skeletal and so removed from the robust cherubic-like child he had been, had finally given the world the option to ignore his misdeeds, his over-spending, his drug use, and his scandalous behaviors.

He had given the world a final performance - one that would wipe his tainted slate clean - one that would allow him to rise out of the mire he made of his life and ride new waves of esteem and veneration - one that would crescendo him into virtual saintdom: an extraordinary, untimely, unrehearsed death.

But he was always and ever just a kid.   A very, very sad confused disturbed talented little kid.

LIFE HAS TO BE HARD

Mary Lou Edwards

Life has to be hard. Not life *was* hard or life *is* hard or life *can be* hard. No, *life has to be hard.*

Experiencing the Great Depression as a teen-ager, my father observed the travails of the jobless. Land mines of economic destruction and desperation exploded around him, wounding his sense of security, and also hurting those who would later share his life. The Depression, the economic vulnerability, were proof that God wanted life to be hard - its psychic imprint served as a constant reminder of His wrath.

From 1932 forward, good, beauty and accomplishment were viewed through astigmatic eyes that dared not allow the celebration of life's achievements. Hard work was the protectant; enjoyment the enemy.

He acknowledged God's gifts, but could not savor them because life had to be a struggle and the Great Scorekeeper kept a sharp eye out for those who searched for the easy way. A God who deprived the undeserving, punished the ungrateful and exacted a price from those who didn't use their gifts correctly was not to be crossed. And because some people were not listening, despite Matthew, Mark, Luke and John having spread The Word, He deputized Jim, and Jim, my father, became God's translator.

Dad interpreted what God meant - what God intended - what God wanted. His pipeline was direct; he understood what God demanded even before God knew, and, because the Deity was preoccupied with wreaking economic havoc around the world and sorting through the wreckage, Dad, familiar with the drill, filled the vacuum. Whether a trifling matter or major issue, he never strayed from the message - life has to be hard.

One didn't really know how to drive unless the car was stick shift nor eat a genuine sandwich unless the bread was homemade. A four-inch footing was insufficient for a proper concrete patio, a three foot pit had to be dug. A week's vacation involved mending screen doors, fixing appliances, and repairing squeaky floor boards in a rented summer cottage. Picnics required home baked cakes and hauling four-course meals a mile, under scorching sun and over burning sand, down to the beach. Because in order to really live, life had to be hard. The tougher it was, the better one was, the closer one came to earning life's gifts and God's approval.

Swimming, biking, ice skating, chess were not pastimes; they were skills to be perfected through effort and practice. Hobbies were a waste of time unless one intended to incorporate them into a career.

College students, according to dad's Gospel, needed to study two hours a night for each scheduled credit hour. In response to his constant badgering that I was a bogus scholar, who really didn't value, care about, want, appreciate or all of the above, an education, I attempted to reason with him.

"Dad," I tried to explain, "I carry 16 hours a semester. I'd have to study 32 hours a night."

"Do you think they're just going to hand you a diploma? Do you think life is a cakewalk?" he responded. "There is no easy way out!"

How silly of me to think good grades indicated sufficient study when only blood, sweat, and tears provided validation. How stupid to forget life was a bitch.

When life got too good, as sometimes happened, Dad would temper it with shame. Shame was the antidote to toxic enjoyment. Shame was the "go to" emotion that ensured one never forgot that life had to be hard.

As a kid, my brother was a good baseball player. He did not brag about it, but he made the fatal mistake of being comfortable with his competence, of knowing he had skill and talent. Life was good for a 12 year-old gifted athlete - maybe too good. He needed to be cut down to size. He had to pay for his adolescent cockiness. God had to teach him, and the great translator would deliver the news.

Once during a ballgame, my brother knocked the winning run out of the park. Thrilled with his accomplishment, he sauntered around the bases basking in the admiration of the crowd. My father was incensed and awaited him at home plate. Yanking my brother by the shirt, he shouted, "Who do you think you are? You need to hustle, move your ass around that field - run like you mean it!"

One can only imagine the embarrassment and humiliation my brother felt at being criticized and ridiculed in front of the crowd. But God wasn't finished - sometimes life had to be extra hard.

Grabbing my brother by the uniform, God dragged him over to the coach. "Don't count that run in the score," He ordered. That homerun doesn't count. The kid didn't earn it, he doesn't appreciate it," he insisted. "Take it off the board!"

It was no longer about the winning homerun. It was about God running amok.
Actually, it was my brother's fault; he'd forgotten that life had to be hard. God had no choice but to teach him a lesson he'd never forget.

Dad continued to carry the message everywhere and never missed an opportunity to educate us about life's trials. No event was too trivial or grand to ruin - one really didn't *deserve* to be on the honor roll, dinner time was for eating not *chattering*, a degree from a world-class institution was *a fluke.*

As I grew, I started to question my father's "no matter what you do it's never good enough and you must always work harder" ethic. Despite his thinking we kids hadn't worked hard enough for the honor roll, we consistently made it so it couldn't have been by chance.   Most degrees were hard won.   We might have gotten lucky;   then again, maybe our best was all that was necessary.

And then I heard about Louie Aparicio hitting a homerun and swaggering around the bases at a White Sox game, and I realized that life didn't have to be hard - that life is only as hard as you make it. Sometimes being good is enough.   Maybe human beings weren't supposed to be perfect.

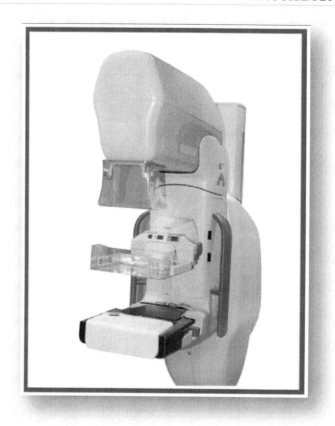

MAMMOGRAM 2009

Carolyn B Healy

4:23 am

Fear penetrates my dream – trapped in a warehouse with endless stairs and no door. I awake with sweaty palms and dread. Dream fades. Whew. Reality invades. Shit. Mammogram Day.

6:00 am

Shower, no deodorant.

6:25 am

Check email. Do not make To Do list for day, just in case.

6:45 am

Take two Extra-Strength Tylenol. Ha! Outwit the flesh-squeezing bastards.

7:00 am
Remove envelope of old films from closet shelf, safer at my house ever since the year they misplaced (and eventually found) them, making it all worse. Do not look at them.

7:05 am
Drive. Park.

7:10 am
Take elevator to 4th floor. Enter office. Go to bathroom. Complete paperwork. Pretend to watch Good Morning America present the various tragedies that occurred overnight while I thought only of myself. Go to bathroom again.

7:25 am
Follow receptionist to changing room. Choose locker # 11. Strip to waist, don enormous pink-flowered flannel gown with many strings. Wrap tight. Sit in waiting room. More Good Morning America. Maintain cocktail party-style chit chat with other patients. Do not mention that we are all in the Diagnostic Mammogram wing for some good reason, not downstairs in Routine Mammogram.

7:35 am
Experience strange calm, proving once again that reality in the moment is easier to handle than the anticipation of it.

7:40 am
Follow smiling harmless-looking tech into her chamber. Small, blonde, young, dressed in green print lab wear; efficient, informative, apologetic, low key, all you could ask for.

7:45 am
Begin on right side. Take arm out of sleeve. Step forward. Stare through blinds as a woman closes her car door, walks away, approaches building, turns around, returns to car for a forgotten bag, repeats.

7:53 am
Follow directions. Stand here. Lean in. Hold this bar. Relax the shoulder. Sorry. Hold breath. Switch to left side.

8:04 am
Almost done. Just the magnified ones of the incision site to go.

8:08 am

Return to waiting room. Wait. Wait longer. Fight off growing conviction that something is wrong.

8:18 am

Large woman enters, comments to no one in particular that she hasn't had one of these things in years. Say something encouraging. Look away. Read magazine.

8:20 am

Watch interview with Bernie Madoff's longtime assistant who had no idea anything was wrong. Believed him. Needed job.

8:23 am

Imagine B. Madoff's male parts compressed between the clear plastic paddles of the mammogram equipment. Would that be torture? Would that be a problem?

8:25 am

Tech returns at last, asks me to follow her into changing room. Oh no – why can't she tell me out here?

>   **Tech**: *It was fine*

>   **Me**: *What a relief. Now, why didn't I just say Good? Why reveal my private torment?*

>   **Tech**: *Here's your paperwork. We'll see you next year.*

>   **Me**: *Yes. Good. Recall that in previous years they'd given out a carnation to commemorate a good outcome. Budget cuts no doubt. The year it wasn't okay I can't remember much, which is just as well. There was no flower, that's for sure.*

>   **Tech**: *Do you want to wait for your films?*

>   **Me**: *Yes. Thanks.*

8:30 am

Dress, return key. Smile. Exhale. Sit in waiting room away from TV. Study other patients. Wonder about percentages: How many get bad news: One in three? Ten? Two hundred?

8:32 am

Check Blackberry.   Read notice of Elizabeth Edwards on book tour. Think about timing: mine early, Stage 0; hers late, too late. Think of her children, so young.

8:35 am

Make list for the day: Breakfast out, Drop off donations to resale shop, Clean patio furniture, Buy plants. Appreciate.

8:45 am

Descend in elevator, films in hand. Escape. Dial the important people. Celebrate another whole beautiful year.

IF WE COULD DO IT OVER

*You need to claim the events in your life
in order to make yourself yours.*

~ Anne Wilson Schaef ~

CONFESSIONS OF A SERIAL FORWARDER

Mary Lou Edwards

God grant me the serenity to accept the things I cannot change,
The courage to change the things I can,
And the wisdom to never forward another email as long as I live...

I am done. Finished. Fini.

I will never pass on another funny joke, lifesaving tip, critical warning or virus threat. Call me selfish, but I'll not even pass on a Code Red Alarm.

I will no longer be the Paul Revere of the Internet. I will not attempt to brighten anyone's day nor feel compelled to tell acquaintances that, like a thousand helium balloons, their friendship lifts my heart. I will not pass along Amber Alerts or Novenas to St. Dymphna, patron of the psychologically impaired.

I was never an irresponsible forwarder. I regularly snopesed things that came my way. If I got an email that claimed women who'd had breast augmentation survived the Titanic because their breasts served as life jackets, I verified it before hitting the SEND button.

I didn't fall for the promises of a cash windfall stuffed in my next Whopper Burger if I said a certain prayer for our soldiers in Iraq. I didn't believe I would contract leprosy if I let the flame on the Candle for World Peace, which has been circulating on the net since October 8, 1952, burn out.

I only disseminated material that would cheer-up shut-ins, brighten the days of the depressed or enlighten the imprudent who gave me their email addresses. I didn't shot-gun messages to my 174 best friend contact list. Rather, I meticulously tailored my forwards to special interest groups - recipes to the Julia Child devotees, Amber Alerts to those who cared about their children, warnings to pet lovers about tainted cat food from China.

I didn't betray confidences about my friends' husbands who were undergoing sex-change surgeries or blabber about my manager's son who was working his way through mortuary school by selling crystal meth.

In short, I was cyber responsible which is why this slip has shattered me.

My friend, an ex-nun, forwarded a story about two old ladies in a nursing home. It was not in the best of taste. I judiciously selected several girlfriends who enable my forwarding addiction and carefully clicked bcc (blind carbon copy) so no one else would know of their morbid fear of drooling away their golden years. I wanted to reassure them that, despite qualifying for Long Term Care Insurance, they need never surrender their prurient perspectives. I took every precaution. I didn't want to be known as the reckless forwarder, one whose name on the

You've Got Mail screen prompts DELETE. I abhor indiscriminate forwarders who willy-nilly send pictures of nursing baby cows, never once considering whether or not the recipient is into bovines.

I am prolific, but selective except for this one freaking time I goofed up. *My, oh my, you do have quite a sense of humor!*

Please, God, no, I thought as I stared in horror at the computer screen. In a flash, I realized that, in my forwarding frenzy to get this oh, so important joke out, I had bcc'ed the name directly above my friend Sue Grote's, and sent the story to a professional acquaintance - a very reserved, genteel minister/psychotherapist.

"George," I shouted as I ran up to our bedroom, "you are not going to believe this - I am mortified. Wake-up! I want to die!"

He continued to snore.

"George," I shrieked, flipping on the light switch and tearing off his blanket, "wake up! I am totally humiliated. I can never show my face again! Get up - this is a disaster."

"Lower your voice and turn off the damn light," he growled, not at all grasping the gravity of the situation. "It's midnight. What the hell is wrong with you?"

"I just got an email from Rev. Grier, Dr. Grier," I cried, kneeling at the side of our bed. "I cannot believe I did this. I am so stupid! I should not be allowed to own a computer. I am an idiot!"

"Could you please save your self-flagellation for the morning? I have to be up at six."

"Oh, you don't care! You don't care that I've just humiliated myself - that I may have to live in a cloister for the rest of my life. Please! Sit up at least," I said, turning the ceiling fan on high to get his attention.

Suddenly it was as though we were in front of a jumbo jet on the tarmac at O'Hare. Olivia, my cat, had come in to investigate the ruckus only to have her long hair blown back as though she were in a wind tunnel.

It worked.

He got up and stomped over to the fan switch almost twisting the knob off the wall. "O.K., O.K. I'm awake. I do care. I'm very interested in why you're suicidal."

"I accidentally forwarded a really, really offensive email to Dr. Grier. I mean really offensive! I'm so embarrassed I could die!"

"I warned you about sending that shit out all the time. Why do you insist on forwarding that crap?"

"I can't help that I'm easily amused and besides, it's not crap - they're little jokes that just might bring a bit of sunshine into people's lives."

"Sunshine?" he exclaimed as though I'd announced I was a crystal meth addict. "If your friends need spam to bring a smile to their faces, they're in bigger trouble than you. Why don't you just stick to sending out computer viruses?"

"Thanks a lot. I'm glad you woke up to tear me down," I said in my best Meryl Streep voice. "I told you it was an accident. Do you think I wanted to send him an email about two old ladies in a nursing home?"

"Old ladies in a nursing home? Are you nuts? Look, I'm sorry if you think I'm tearing you down, but you're a maniac on that computer. It's a wonder you have any friends left who will even open your stuff."

"Well," I said haughtily, "I happen to have 174 friends in my address book. I'll bet you don't have half that."

"Look, I'm not having this stupid ass conversation at this hour. Let's get some sleep."

"Sleep? No, no, listen to me! You haven't heard the joke. It's so outrageous I wish I could go into witness protection," I moaned. "Please, please - just listen to the joke."

"You don't get it! I NEED SLEEP. I don't care about this nonsense! I do not care about your joke. I have a life!"

His insensitivity never ceased to amaze me. I ignored his unreasonable objections.

> Two old ladies in wheelchairs were in a nursing home.
> One old lady asks the other, *"Do you ever get horny?"*
> The other says, *"Yes."*
> So the first old lady says, *"What do you do about it?"*
> And the second old lady says, *"I suck on a Lifesaver."*
> And the first old lady says, *"Who drives you to the beach?"*

For a minute there was dead silence. He stared as though I were a postal worker with a gun. I could tell he was counting to a hundred. Finally he said quietly, "Well, wasn't this a car crash waiting to happen."

And that's why I will never again forward anything as long as I live. I don't care if someone sends me a YouTube of Barbara Bush giving Barack a lap dance, I swear I will not pass it on.

O.K. Maybe I'll call you and give you the URL, but that's it.

ENOUGH ALREADY

Carolyn B. Healy

I quit watching The Today Show on the third day of the Michael Jackson death marathon. If they were going to act like the entire world screeched to a halt just because one exceedingly troubled entertainer died, then they'd have to do it without me. I am not without compassion for M. Jackson, as he was clearly victimized first and repeatedly before he turned his attentions to young boys. I just sought some balance and the slightest recognition that he had become a predator himself.

Soon after, I left on a lengthy trip where my morning viewing switched to the cruise director's daily closed circuit TV show, for which he donned a turban and received a lovely facial from the spa staff, and talked on and on about shopping. I didn't miss Today at all.

Once back, I needed a week to overcome jet lag, and was finally ready to resume my usual habits. Certainly Today was over the pop star immersion by now and back to actual news, so I switched it on. What filled the screen but the entire Duggar family, the reality show crew who unapologetically shows off their incredible flair for reproduction, a 21-person crowd seated somehow - they must have bleachers in the living room - around the parents.

"The Duggars are here. And they have an announcement," the off-screen voiced teased. "We'll be right back."

Let's see . . . this is the Duggars. Whatever could it be? A cure for a deadly disease? Peace in the Middle East? You got it. They are having another frigging baby. Nothing against the baby, who is blameless in all this, but hardly could be considered fortunate, to show up on the doorstep as child # 19. That poor kid will be scrambling for attention until the cows come home. They are going to have to assign someone to remember his name.

Mrs. D announced it in her strangely childlike voice, while the rest of the family stared vacantly, and Mr. D, a John Edwards lookalike, hitched up his belt and tried to look modest. "We are so excited," she warbled, "waiting for our 19th child." Then they chatted with the eldest son's new wife, pregnant of course, about their upcoming birth, and the segment was over.

It's enough to make you look kindly on the Chinese ban on multiple children. And makes you wonder just who is raising whom around the Duggar household. I don't care if both parents permanently gave up sleeping for the next 15 years, there is no way two people can adequately parent 18, now 19, children.

While Mr. and Mrs. D are happily reproducing like rabbits, they conscript their existing children to raise the new ones. It's like a Ponzi scheme for parenting - invest your sperm and egg in this new opportunity, but skim off the resources of other people to make good on it. And act like everything is fine and dandy.

Back in the day when my husband and I formed our notions about family size there was a concept called Zero Population Growth, an early expression of consciousness about how we use the earth. It was based on the ethic that no one family gets to hog more than their fair share of the resources. ZPG guided us down a logical path - just replace yourself and then do a bang-up job of raising your replacements. Lucky for us, it worked out that we had a son and almost three years later, a daughter, so we could carry out that plan.

It wasn't that I was so enraptured with the ecological part of the idea, but as an only child who longed hard for a sibling, two children seemed an embarrassment of riches, and I set out to give them scads of attention and intention.

I gradually noticed that while most of our friends planned their families as we did, some other folks out there still cranked out kids like they needed to raise their own field hands. This ZPG thing had a pull, but not for everyone. Of course, many powerful forces were at work - religion, family tradition, culture, competitiveness, repeated tries for a child of the other sex, fertility, medical issues.

I understand that everyone has to chart their own course, and I have absolutely no patience with those in the anti-choice faction who are ready to make everyone else's reproductive decisions for them. I certainly don't want to join their ranks. But I do have some thoughts.

The more I see these giant families like the Duggars lionized, the more I wonder why. The Duggars can't stop themselves, and parade their lives on TV, looking back at us with smug smiles. I wonder, when they started all of this way back in the 1980's, did they have this planned or did they just sit back and let it happen.

In 1997, the McCaughey Family from Iowa produced septuplets on top of their one existing child. In religiously-loaded interviews, they credited themselves with refusing the selective reduction of the number of fetuses that doctors recommended, and credited their prayers for the survival of all the children. Luckily for them, only two of the children have cerebral palsy. Their self-congratulation aside, what does this say about the prayers of other parents whose babies were stillborn, or died days after birth; or the prayers of infertile couples who would give anything to be pregnant with one measly fetus? Were those prayers less valid, less fervent, less worthy?

And just last year, Octomom, who already had six children, two with special needs, added her eight new babies to the mix. The reaction to her news suggests that we may finally have had enough. As she looked coyly at the camera denying that she was angling for a reality show, the celebrity machinery went wild. While journalists and others climbed all over the lawn and seduced her parents into on-air interviews, ethicists were finally asked to examine the issues involved on air.

All these families grant themselves permission that most of us would responsibly deny. Is all of this self-congratulation and self-promotion the final and most tragic expression of our acquisitiveness? The one who dies with the most children wins?

Or is this just a freak show that serves to entertain the rest of us who would never dream of turning out two baseball teams under our very own roofs - a cautionary tale about what happens when excess overtakes reason? If so, we have circled back to M. Jackson and his sadly overblown life.

Here comes the really touchy part. Internationally, we see reports of countries nearly paralyzed by poverty and disease and scarcity of resources. Yet their average family sizes would put them in the running for a TV show on cable. From here, it looks pretty easy to solve. Apply ZPG and you turn an unmanageable situation into a workable one. Sounds logical to me.

But that brings a minefield of potentially explosive issues. Dare to speak of limiting population and you risk charges of colonialism, racism, classism. But reality is clear - producing too many people makes life harder, and in those extreme situations, even impossible to sustain.

At our house, we did what seemed right and it worked out fine. There is the occasional twinge, wondering what it would have been like to throw ZPG to the winds and be surrounded now by many more children. Just like there is the occasional twinge for others who wonder what it would have been like to mount a huge career, or set aside material comforts and go out to save the world. That is what we get to do as life moves along, review our lives and sort out the hard-won wisdom from the regrets.

All other things being equal, like love and plenty to eat, surely there are riches to be had in enormous families that I will never know. And surely there is a quality of connection in small families that the Duggars will never know.

Now, I have to decide what to do about my relationship with the Today Show. I'm pretty sure I know what I'll do - I'll tune back in. I have a curiosity problem. I can't wait to see what they come up with next.

HAPPILY EVER AFTER

Ellie Searl

And . . . they lived happily ever after. THE END

"Night, night, sweetie girl, sleep tight."

"How do you know?"

"How do I know what?"

"That they liveded happily ever after."

"*Lived*, not *liveded*. Well, they just did, like in all your other stories."

"Bambi's mommy didn't. She got shotted by a mean hunter."

"**Shot**, not *got shotted*."

"And the poor little match girl got *frozed*."

"Just say *froze*."

"But they got *dead*! *They* didn't lived happily ever after."

"You mean they *died*, not *got dead*. And say 'they didn't *live* happily ever after,' not *lived* - well, true, they didn't, but that's not how you say it."

"What about the blinded mice? Their tails were cutted right *off* . . . with a carvenife . . . what's a carvenife?"

"*Blind* mice. It's *blind*, not *blinded*. Say *cut* off. It was a carv*ing* knife, not carven - like the one we use to slice our roast beef with."

"She chopted their tails off with her *meat* cutterer?"

"*Chopped* their tails off . . . with a meat *cutter* . . . oh my, . . . yes . . . she did."

"Why? Did she *hated* the mice? Were they *bad*?"

"You mean, did she *hate* the mice. I suppose she didn't like the mice very much. They must have been very, very bad mice. Let's tuck you in now."

"Did they bleeded?"

"Did what bleeded? . . . bleed . . . . It's *bleed*."

"The mice tails."

"They probably bled. Now go to sleep."

"How much?"

"How much what?"

"Did they bled?"

"*Bleed*! It's *bleed*. Probably only a little."

"Did they got band-aids?"

"*Get* band-aids. Yes, yes, . . . ok, now here's where you can say *got*. They *got* band-aids. I imagine they got band-aids."

"From *who*?"

"*Whom*! Say *from whom*. Their mother, I suppose. Now good night."

"What about me?"

"What about you?"

"Are you going to chopted *me* up if *I'm* bad?"

"*Chop*. Not . . . *chopted!* No, honey, I'm not going to hurt you, ever."

"Will I live happily ever after?"

"What? Oh, of course you will. You'll be the happiest big girl in the world. Ok, that's all for tonight."

"You aren't."

"Hmm?"

"You aren't."

"Aren't what?"

"Happy."

"I'm not?

"No. You shout at Muffin and you tell me to wipe my face in a meany voice and you get mad at Daddy when he helpted you wrong . . . and . . . sometimes . . . you cry."

"Look . . . Sweetie . . . I love you and Daddy very much . . . but, every now and then, I might get upset . . . just a teeny bit . . . but that doesn't mean I'm not happy. You'll see someday. You really do need to go to sleep now. And it's not *helpted* me. It's *helped*."

"*Where* does the prince and princess lived happily ever after?"

"*Do live* . . . I mean . . . *did live* . . . they *lived* . . . Oh, Lord, . . . ok . . . they *did live* in a castle.

"Did the prince *helped* the princess?"

"*HELP!* It's *HELP!* . . . *did help* the princess. Yes, he . . . well, ok . . . now you can say **helped**. . . . . He **helped** her . . . all the time . . . mm mmm."

"I hope they getted a dog."

"*Don't say getted*! . . . . Say **got!** Yes, they **got** a very, very magnificent dog."

"What *kind* of dog? Like Muffin?"

"Yes, absolutely! Exactly like Muffin."

"Read it again, Mommy."

"Tomorrow night. It's late. Now, good*night*."

I kissed her forehead and turned out the light, feeling a little sad and very much like going to bed myself. *Tomorrow night, I'll just stick with the story.*

"Mommy?"

"Mm?"

"Does they ever *got* a *cat*?"

SUCCESS AND FAILURE

*If at first you don't succeed, try, try again. Then quit.
No sense being a damn fool about it.*

~ W.C. Fields ~

SUCCESS AND FAILURE - CUBAN STYLE

Carolyn B Healy

Celia got us there with 20 minutes to spare. We collected on the open-air platform and looked around. On the earth road alongside, we witnessed a few centuries' worth of transportation options whiz by. A horse and cart carried a local man hauling a sack of grain; another cart hauled a tourist couple also rushing to make the train. A bicycle rickshaw scooted by, carrying a local woman dressed for the office, although looking around the very small town, it was hard to see where she might be headed. A series of 1950-era Chevys and DeSotos and a couple of rusty

Ford pickups also buzzed by while we waited. A mid-1960's Soviet Lada, a boxy successor imported once Fidel shut down the supply of the U.S. cars, followed. Cash for Clunkers would be an enormous hit in Cuba if only anyone had any money, or the right to buy a new car.

Early that morning, after a sumptuous brunch at the hotel, Celia had urged us onto our luxurious Chinese bus for our trip into the countryside. Maximo sat at the wheel, greeting each rider with nods and a wordless smile. Maximo spoke no English, we were told. We had also been told that Celia, like all guides, would have to watch her words, as you never know who might disapprove and turn her in to the state for unauthorized opinions. That was enough to get us all to keep an eye on Maximo and his motives (How did we really know he speaks no English?), and nervous that our endearing single mother new friend Celia would overstep her boundaries.

She kept us moving all morning, afraid we would miss our connection. Today our tour was to show us the remnants of the greatest of the Cuban crops, sugar, and of the lifestyle it provided for those involved. Into her microphone, as we sped along the National Highway, she described Cuba's relationship with sugar over the years from the lynchpin of the economy to the near collapse of the industry with the end of slavery, and its transfer to the hands of U.S. companies in the years before Fidel showed up and nationalized the companies. It limped into the 1980's, but once the Soviets collapsed themselves and could no longer be any help with fuel or machinery, it faded further.

We waited on the platform, guiltily snapping photos of modest residents' daily lives as if we were viewing an ancient culture sprung to life. They want us here, we comforted ourselves; they want us to see how they live and take home evidence so others will know. Or at least they'd like to get a good look at some Americans, the folks they are forbidden to mix with, except on the four hours of nightly U.S. television shows. I can't figure out the motivation of the regime to welcome Brothers and Sisters and Two and a Half Men into the struggling lives of the Cuban people. Was it to highlight the decadent empty materialistic lives of the capitalist pigs? Or to provide the barest hint of freedom, a nightly secret pleasure to keep the masses reassured that they are not so isolated after all? Even with a nightly drip of American media, how much does the average Cuban know of life outside the island? Deprived of CNN, Internet access and travel, yet taunted by fictional lives set in Malibu and Ohai, CA, what must they imagine?

Cubans are accustomed to fiction, being raised on a steady diet of claims about the success of the Revolution despite mountains of evidence to the contrary. They receive lectures about agrarian reform while tractors rust in untended fields. They hear about the glories of the generous food rationing system while they dash out the back door to their black market suppliers to gather enough for the family to eat. They are told about the fine highways that crisscross the countryside while they congregate in intersections waiting for hours for trucks to provide stand-up rides to cities outside Havana, because no one making the monthly wage of under $20 can possibly afford a $17 bus ride to a mid-island city.

Cuba has a history of occupation and domination by outside powers. There was always someone coming along to overpower and exploit the Cuban people and strip their resources - a parade of Spaniards, English, French, and yes, Americans.

When the first wave, the Spaniards, showed up in search of gold, they managed to wipe out the indigenous population in a quick 30 years, with European diseases, overwork and mass suicide. This created an opening and a business opportunity for the African slave trade to begin, which continued to the tune of 400,000 individuals before it was done. That was the constant, while the nationality of the colonists rotated, along with the crops they worked - tobacco, sugar, whatever. There was always wealth to be had, but it seemed to slip through the fingers of ordinary Cubans and land right in the pockets of the already rich and favored families of whichever world power was in charge at the time.

When the train arrived, the locomotive chugging and belching steam, we climbed into its open-air cars and settled into polished wooden seats. Celia wrangled the last few of us who had wandered off to get just one more picture of the dusty town.

The train inched out of the station and began its slow climb up the valley that had once been the center of the world's sugar production. As we began to build up speed, a man dressed in a striped shirt, gripping a guitar, appeared from one of the lanes. He sprinted hard after the train and leapt onto its back platform, grabbing the bar just in time. He strode up the aisle and joined his musical partner waiting with trumpet in hand, and they struck up the Afro-Cuban rhythm we could hear in our sleep.

In the back of the car, another passenger, a young Cuban woman dressed in a white blouse and flowing skirt danced in the aisle with her young friend. He soon tired and an older man stepped up, eager to match her swiveling hips to his. Minutes later, they fell into their seats, satisfied, while the musicians played on. The tourists applauded.

The music never stops in Cuba. At every venue a group pounded out the rhythm and sang until we were out of sight. From our hotels we could hear the pulse of the clubs far into the night. Sometimes there were horns, always guitars and drums, and the voices. Even if we couldn't understand the words, we knew what they sang about - longing and heat and sex. We could tell that much.

As we proceeded up the valley we passed the occasional house surrounded by tidy garden plots. Mostly we saw expanses of untended fields with remnant sugar cane plants sprouting from dry and cracked soil. When we saw workers, they held machetes or followed oxen pulling a plow. It looked like Fidel's grand plan for agrarian reform hadn't quite taken hold.

It was all pretty in a sad way, crisp clouds against a bright blue sky, the hilly landscape still green but raggedy. It was easy to imagine the best years, the growers and their families traveling from their grand Havana homes to the opulent country houses, chugging up the valley to watch the harvest of their wealth.

It got even easier to imagine once we climbed off the train and walked up a slope to one of those country houses, restored to Victorian grandeur with crystal chandeliers and shaded porches. Outside, a market was set up to lure the tourists, full of embroidered clothing and linens and eager vendors chasing down tourists to view their wares. It was one of the few displays of crass commercialism we witnessed.

To escape their pleas, I wandered beyond the stalls. A tower rose from the dusty earth. Architecturally interesting, its stacks of winding staircases and arches invited picture-taking. After snapping a series of artsy shots featuring rolling fields framed by the tower's arches, I looked up. What was this thing for anyway? Oh. Of course. A slave tower, built so that the overseers could keep track of who was working hard enough and who was not, and to make sure no one escaped. It focused my attention on the other side of the commercial equation, and interfered with my appreciation of the wealth and luxury that had flowed from the sugar trade.

The slaves arrived from many African tribes over 300-plus years to do the work, at one point accounting for 45% of the population. About a third of them were headed for the plantations, the rest for house slave spots. Over the years, a series of rebellions broke out, the first in 1513, but the system chugged on unabated until outlawed in 1886.

Cuban slavery had some particular features that sound good: a slave could take three days off to try to find a better owner, where he could negotiate his own price and the price of his eventual freedom. Yes, the slave had a potential out, if he could raise enough money to buy his freedom. Some did, and became middle class slave-owners themselves, a spectacular failure of imagination in my book.

Before we start handing out human rights awards, the other facts scream of what we normally associate with slavery. Slaves rarely were allowed to marry, families who arrived together were torn apart, babies born to strong healthy young women were taken to be nursed by other slaves bred for the purpose.

All the success, the riches, the opulence came from a failure of humanity that allowed this systematic exploitation, a violation of decency and fairness. Did all the flaunting of wealth and competitive spending we'd seen throughout Cuba, from the marble burial vaults to the elegant carriages and fancy houses, help answer some of our questions about Fidel's success here, and the Cubans' apparent reluctance to oppose him? Did the long history of exploitation begin to explain Fidel's ascendance as the hero of everybody gets the same and nobody better try to outdo their neighbors?

We climbed back on the train for the return trip, heads full of the competing agendas of the colonists, industrialists, slaves and revolutionaries. Cuba shut down the sugar mills five years ago, giving up the fantasy of reviving the glory days. It seems just as well.

EXIT CENTER STAGE

Ellie Searl

Perhaps I shouldn't have resigned.

Drama and my life have been a tight weave since words began to cascade from my imagination. I told stories with great flair - performing stream-of-consciousness sagas, updating the adventures of my characters-du-jour. They somersaulted when excited, stomped when frustrated, danced when amused, wailed when upset, shrieked when scared, and pouted when ignored, which was often, due to failure of the audience to remain as interested in my stories as I. Center stage. I thrived on center stage.

For years, my mother called me a pest. I heard it often in one guise or another. "Stop your blather." "Quit being a nuisance." "Be more like your brothers - they don't annoy people." Once she called me histrionic. I thought that was a compliment.

I was in my first play was when I was six, cast as an apple tree, draped in brown and green crepe paper with red felt dots. I stood erect under the

August sun with my bent limbs held in position for the length of the play, sweat dripping down my tummy making me itch. I wanted to be Alice – the lead - but Karen, Miss Alpha Pants, a doctor's daughter who always got what she wanted, played that part. Besides, the show was in her back yard, and it was directed by her mother, who also made the white cupcakes with orange icing. In time, I learned to accept that there are no small parts, just small actors. Often it's the small role that's noteworthy. Take Robert Duvall. He played Boo Radley in *To Kill a Mockingbird*. All he did was stand behind a door. Mute. Like a tree.

In high school, I played Mammy – in blackface. Highly non-PC today, but at the time it wasn't considered objectionable. There was one African American family in our town of 800, but even the eldest child wasn't yet a Freshman, so he wouldn't have qualified. No one would have asked him anyway because *that* would have been considered objectionable.

It was when I moved to Ohio that I became active in "living room" theater. Once a month our friends gathered in someone's home and read a play, acting it out - complete with costumes and props. My first part with this ensemble was Margot Wendice in *Dial M for Murder*. I performed my role without a hitch, holding the script in my left hand and scissors in my right, so my character could cut coupons from a newspaper.

Our "troupe" wasn't a group of aspiring actors - just people who loved theater. Performance-challenged Bill played Inspector Hubbard. He read his part in a monotone, pondering over each syllable as though it had some dramatic significance. But it was reading his own stage directions that threw Hitchcock into a graveyard tailspin. *"So, Mrs. Wendice, exactly why did you stab Swann with the scissors? Parenthesis turns to Mrs. Wendice holding the scissors in his handkerchiefed hand parenthesis."*

Sandy, a member of our local community theater happened to be at that play reading. She said I was a natural and should check out the Mahoning Valley Community Theater.

I was somewhat familiar with MVCT. The building was beautiful and spacious and gracious: a large lobby with plush red carpet, mahogany paneled walls covered with photographs of past productions, and an easel holding headshots of the actors in the current play. The proscenium stage looked out onto a semi-circle of seating for over 1000 people.

Backstage had rooms, nooks, and crannies designed specifically for props or costumes or rehearsals or carpentry. The separate dressing rooms for men and women had counters and seats for 10 actors each, with lighted mirrors for make-up and hair. This might have been small community theater, but the facility sent off a big-city theater vibe. And I wanted to be part of it.

Within the week, I was at the theater introducing myself and dropping Sandy's name all over the place. Within two weeks, I had a foot in the door as an intermission hostess.

From the outside the theater seemed vigorous – a spirited force. It didn't take long to feel the strong undertow eroding its soul.

MVCT at intermission was a performance in itself. The attempt at elegance resembled afternoon tea with the Duchess of Excess. Oak tables, red gilded table runners, tiered candelabras, ruffled paper tart-cups filled with shell-shaped shortbread cookies, towering brass pull-handle urns full of decaffeinated coffee, and heavy cut-glass punch bowls loaded with a sticky foam concoction of raspberry sherbet and Sprite, chilled by a Jello-mold ice ring. I swallowed my love of simplicity, ladled the garish goo into glass cups, and sashayed my way through the crowd with trays of cookies.

But I wanted the stage, and the lobby wasn't the stage. So I played my role of hostess with enough syrupy sweetness to refill the punch bowls, hoping Important Theater People would notice my charm and enthusiasm. I wasn't aware that I was breaking Rule #1.

To participate in any type of MVCT event, even serving cookies at intermission, a volunteer needed be a season ticket holder. And to be considered for an on-stage role, a volunteer also needed to be a graduate of Acting Forum I, the theater's two-week September orientation and acting class, led by the director himself. Acting Forum II, held six months later, was not required, but it was encouraged, advocated, promoted, underscored, and expected, if the actor wanted credibility, respect, and first-name rapport with any of the Regulars.

It wasn't until I returned a borrowed theater prop to a died-in-the-wool, rule-abiding, finger-shaking theater veteran that I learned of my major indiscretion. She padded to her front door.

"Hi," I said. "I'm Ellie - from the theater. I'm returning your vase."

She straightened a bit. Her eyes burned into mine. "Hm! You Searl?"

Where was the thank you? The smile? This wasn't what I expected.

"Yes, Ellie Searl."

"You don't have a season ticket," she croaked. "You're not supposed to work at the theater until you have a season ticket." She snatched the vase from my hand.

My throat slammed shut. I managed to choke a weak, "I . . . I'm just helping . . . with intermission . . . ah . . . setting up . . . serving. Sandy is a friend of . . ."

"Doesn't matter. You want to work at the theater, you get a ticket." Her chin slumped into her chest as she shut the door, leaving me on her front porch like yesterday's trash.

When I reported the incident to the volunteer supervisor, I expected to hear gossip-stories about the old bag. But I was chastised - again.

"What? You don't have a season ticket? You're not supposed to work at the theater until you have a season ticket. So until you get one, you can't be a hostess."

This was Serious Business. My desire to have an acting part overtook common sense. I bought a season ticket, signed up for Forum I, reserved a spot in Forum II, volunteered for the costume committee, and reinstated myself as intermission hostess, sticky punch notwithstanding. I figured I'd better do things according to protocol if I wanted credibility, respect, and first-name rapport with any of the Regulars.

That's when I discovered Rule #2. Parts for all play productions were invitation only. MVCT did not have auditions. Any actor aspiring to have an on-stage role - speaking, non-speaking, statue, sauce pan - was sent a letter that revealed the upcoming play and urged the recipient to participate. The letter did not tell the recipient what part he or she would have. It could be the maid. It could be the lead. It could be Boo Radley behind the door. These invitations came from the Script and Cast Council, the Supreme Court of MVCT - whose members continued serving until they died, moved away, or were sent to a home.

The anonymous members of the SCC evaluated prospective actors' stage presence and acting ability by sneaking in on Forum I and Forum II sessions and taking notes. I could see them lurking in the shadows of the empty theater seats while the class worked on the techniques of voice projection and vowel pronunciation. They sat in the darkened corners of the top rows with their spiral notebooks, coils shimmering red and gold from Exit signs and stage lights. *These mysterious creatures are my future in this theater,* I thought. *How do I appear to them? Is my voice strong enough? Are my a's and o's round enough? Will I ever be in a play? Will I ever receive THE LETTER?*

During the first forum, I met some lovely people with whom I developed a comfortable relationship. Whenever I bumped into one of them, I felt welcomed. But the Regulars, I discovered, were a different breed altogether. Forget the credibility, respect, and first-name rapport. Getting recognition from the prima donnas of MVCT was like trying to toss water through a wall of glass. Those Experienced Actors fed each other's egos and padded their own self-importance under the pretext of theater loyalty. During breaks in rehearsals they talked about the good-old-days when people, themselves included, of course, really understood what real theater was all about – when actors were "off book" before the third run-through, or when actors were so good they didn't need voice lessons, or when cast parties were fun. "Not like today," they'd say, "when everybody and his uncle wants to be on stage, but can't act their way through a rat hole." No, I wasn't comfortable with the Regulars.

I repaired and pressed costumes, organized outfits on backstage racks, assisted with quick changes, and stayed late to clean up. But I was an underling and didn't warrant recognition by the actors who had more important things to consider – like their write-ups in the playbook or their headshots on the lobby wall.

One afternoon, I received a letter from the SCC inviting me to play a role in *Twelve Angry Women.* Thrilled to be asked, I removed everything from my personal calendar that interfered with rehearsals six days a week for six weeks and three long weekends of production after that.

I loved everything about the on-stage portion of the production. I learned my part quickly, followed the directors' instructions, and acted well, I thought. I thrived on playing someone else night after night, allowing my character to take charge of my life for a few hours, stepping into my character's soul and letting it lead me through the imaginary world of the playwright until the curtain fell. What a charge it was being "other-personed."

The director gave me very few wrap-up notes after rehearsals or performances.. Every now and then he'd make a suggestion, but there were virtually no other comments - negative or positive. I asked a Regular why the director didn't give much feedback about my on-stage performance.

She said, "If he doesn't give you notes, he likes what you're doing. Don't look for compliments. You'll get a big head."

Droves of big heads roamed the theater. I wanted to answer, "Like you?" but didn't.

Despite joining the ranks of those who had received an on-stage role, backstage was as uncomfortable as ever. The Clique of Regulars held court, and the Others, like me, stayed in their corners waiting until approached to take part in conversation.

Once I volunteered to be a Director's Assistant for Steve, one of the Regulars, who was invited by the SCC to direct a one-act play for the little theater-in-the-round. Steve was a terrible actor. My husband and I had seen him play the lead in Neil Simon's *Chapter Two*. Stiff, robot-like gestures, monotone delivery – emoting less passion than a throw rug. Ed and I left at intermission while those who could stick it out elevated their sugar levels on liquid treacle. I couldn't imagine Mr. Wretched directing others and making it a decent production.

For six weeks as Steve's assistant, I sat beside him, followed the script, cued the actors, took notes, checked on props, and located costumes. I even prepared a dress rehearsal feast of bagels, veggie spreads, and coffee. "Good job, Ellie," I congratulated myself after opening night. The play was a disaster, but the costumes and props looked good.

A week later, Steve passed me in the hall, stopped, looked at me with a slight squint, and said, "Can I help you?" in a tone that really meant, *What the hell are you, a stranger, doing, running amok in my theater, where everyone else around here is a Regular, and you aren't?*

"I'm Ellie – Ellie Searl."

No reaction.

"I was your *DIRECTOR'S ASSISTANT* for last weekend's production."

"Oh. Right. Hi." And off he went.

Had Steve not been such a terrible actor, I might have dissolved into the linoleum, but by then I had realized that the Clique of Regulars, those people I had so envied and wanted to be like, consisted mainly of acting automatons, like Steve, who hadn't learned their craft at all, or if they had, they had forgotten the main concepts of verisimilitude, voice control, natural stage gestures, pacing – all those skills that hold people in their seats beyond intermission. The Regulars flouted the notion of self-improvement. Repeating Forum I or II? Putting themselves under the scrutiny of the Script and Cast Council? Ridiculous. Those classes were for amateurs.

The director frequently gave notes to the Regulars. "Show more emotion." or "I want to *believe* you're angry." or "Don't *sway* when you speak. You're not HOLDING A BABY!" I flashed my high school play - unskilled teenaged thespians sing-songing their way through the script, stomping for emphasis, flailing their arms without purpose.

What I didn't understand was how the Regulars continued, season after season, to buffalo the SCC into thinking those stage fixtures were still worthy of lead roles. Probably the director wished like hell he could hold auditions - cull the old-timers from the list.

MVCT was built on a foundation of antiquated tradition, which hadn't been evaluated in decades. Loyalty to the theater's dead founder was strong, and no one had the where-with-all to challenge her design. The theater was haunted by long-departed big-city theater wannabes: their footsteps creaking stage floorboards, their apparitions spewing tucked-in-the-attic-thinking.

Yes, the building was beautiful and spacious and gracious, and, if used according to physical design, had great potential in developing a welcoming stage for the community. But as long as the Powers that Be held onto the old rituals and continued to dilute the spirit of new blood, the theater would be a shell - without heart and without passion. Eventually I came to accept that community wasn't a priority and probably wouldn't be for a very long time. So, after a five-year love-hate relationship, I severed ties with the Mahoning Valley Community Theater.

Sometimes I regret giving up that real-theater rush of on-stage performance. I continue with the occasional play readings in people's homes. Just last September I played Sister Aloysius in *Doubt*. It was a hoot being an irate nun vying for the removal of Father Flynn, an alleged pedophile priest.

Every so often, when I return to Ohio for visits, I run into a Regular from the theater. We're polite, but there is a lingering tension and a slight sting, the kind one feels when a small wound is exposed to the air.

I played a variety of roles at MVCT, both center and back stage. Some were big, some were small, and some were barely visible. I even stood behind the door

In retrospect, I am glad to be out of the shadows. If you see Boo, tell him I said 'Hey.'

DON'T BE CRUEL

Mary Lou Edwards

"Ma'am," the lady from the Visitors Center responded, "This is Elvis Week. There ain't a room for miles around - not even one with a bathtub never mind a swimmin' pool. Why the whole town is jam-packed. Fans come from all over the world."

Welcome to Graceland, a place we'd managed to avoid but finally agreed to visit thanks to the relentless badgering of Gianna, our 12 year-old Elvis groupie. Elvis had been dead since 1977. Twenty years later, I assumed he'd have very few fans left so I made no advance hotel reservations.

Having driven the last 400 miles in a rain storm, "no room at the inn" was the last thing I needed to hear. I had four little girls in tow, our daughters, Gianna and Lia and their friends twelve-year old Amy and seven year-old Elise. They'd been good sports for 800 miles, but it was obvious they needed to work off some energy. My husband's twitching eyes suggested he was a bit on edge, and the "are we there yet" and "we're hungry" whines were not helping matters. The single stroke of luck had been that I walked into the Visitors Center alone and no one else heard the dire news. If my husband found out that I'd not booked a hotel during Elvis Week, he'd go absolutely ballistic. I had to get to a phone. *Please, God, take pity on me and come through with a last minute cancellation* I prayed.

I spotted the Family Fun Buffet - a drenched purple dinosaur waved people into the parking lot. "There's Barney!" I cheered, "Let's eat here!" With the sigh of a martyr, George turned into the parking lot.

"Go ahead and get a table while I stop in the Ladies Room," I said as they tore out of the van and streaked through the monsoon. Exiting the van, I slipped and plopped into a puddle. The soggy dinosaur waddled over and giggled, "M'am, let me help you. You look like you're in trouble." *If Barney only knew* I thought.

Limping into the restaurant, I found the Yellow Pages and a phone and dialed six hotels in a row only to hear, "Sorry, booked solid." On the seventh, I hit pay dirt. Yes, they had a room and they were located right across from Graceland! *Is this luck or what?* I thought. It proved to be *or what?*

I found George in the dining area, cradling his head on the table, exhausted from the long stormy drive. Each of the girls was inhaling a plate of desserts - cupcakes, pie, brownies, ice cream, Jell-o and cookies - all smothered in marshmallow fluff.

I winced at George's willingness to let the inmates run the asylum, but something told me I'd be pushing my luck if I started lecturing on nutrition. Instead I herded everyone back to the van and gave George directions to the Graceland Hotel.

"How did you find this place?" my husband asked as we turned into the ominous parking lot. Huge, burly men in uniform surrounded the property. "It looks like they have good security," I observed. "Good security? Are you nuts? They're carrying shot-guns."

"Maybe the hotel wants to discourage the Graceland fans from running across to use the bathrooms."

Later I learned of Graceland's unusual historic odyssey. Long ago, when a local doctor built what was to become Elvis' Graceland, the property was in a very rural area far outside Memphis. Years later when Elvis bought the house, Memphis had grown some, but the area was still a good distance from town and semi-rural. In the last 25 years, however, Memphis had grown by leaps and bounds and Graceland now sat in the middle of a rough, drug-riddled section of the city, but the armed militia did strike me as a bit over the top.

As we entered the hotel, the desk clerk barked, "Whatta you want?" as though we were trespassers. His tattoos suggested he could be an Insane Disciple gangbanger, but his demeanor was more menacing.

"You have a reservation for Edwards?" I asked, gawking at his inch long pinkie nails and the hotel's Early Trailer Park decor.

"Oh, yeah, yer the lady called a few minutes ago. Room for six. That's $400."

"$400? You must be joking," I blurted. Making a quick recovery, I said, "If it's not too much trouble, may we see the room?" We did not need to get on the wrong side of this guy.

"OK," he shrugged, "we'll take the stairs - elevator ain't workin'."

"This place gives me the creeps," George whispered as we made our way up the dingy stairwell. "It's either a drug den or a whorehouse."

"It's convenient to Graceland," I whispered back, "we'll push a dresser in front of the door."

We exited the stairwell, creeping along like a company of moles. The hall smelled of cigars and sweat. The carpeting was threadbare and stained.

When the intimidating desk clerk unlocked the room, the kids tore past us and immediately stripped to their swimsuits. I wanted to accept this room, but a layer of grime covered the bedspread, carpeting and windows.

I had to think of a diplomatic way to back out of this deal without aggravating the frightening thug.

"Girls," I called to the boisterous brood, "we can't stay here. We need more beds," I added, as we made a beeline for the door.

"Stop!" the biker ordered. "You *din't* seen the beds in the adjoining room." The adjoining room was a miniscule closet in which two sets of bunk beds had been crammed. The soiled mattresses had no linens.

"Look," Elise crowed, "a clubhouse!" The older girls scampered up the ladder.

"I figgered they'd like it," the biker remarked. "You git sheets at sign in."

As I sagged into defeat, I remembered the pool.

"Sir, where is the swimming pool?"

"Filled it with *see'ment* during the remodel."

"No swimming pool?" I exclaimed loudly so the girls would hear. Thank God, they did.

They flew out the door chanting *we want to swim . . . you promised . . .* They couldn't have been more appropriately obnoxious if we'd rehearsed.

"They *prolly* covered a few *ho'tel* guests with *see'ment* when they remodeled," George remarked, as we squealed out of the parking lot.

Within minutes, he stopped in front of a *Buy Your Elvis Souvenir Here* store. "I'm running in to buy Graceland tickets," he said. "You did such a great job creating this disaster, think about straightening it out, Sweetie."

Threatening bodily harm if anyone dared leave the van, I found a phone and called the Visitors Center with a gut-wrenching tale that happened to be true - four children, an exhausted husband, a marriage at stake and nowhere to go.

"Well, we do have a special facility for emergency situations," the Greeter drawled. "It's a ho'tel on the outskirts of town that is completely filled up, but during Elvis Week, and only during Elvis Week, Memphis allows them to subdivide their banquet room into small cubicles and put some fold-aways in - that's all I got."

"We'll take it," I said.

"Now, mind you, this is special for Elvis Week since it is against the Memphis Fire Code. The roll-aways are $50 per night. Check-in is at eight and check-out is at eight and there's a swimmin' pool under the escalators in the lobby."

My husband returned. "Did you find a room at Heartbreak Hotel?"

"No, but I found a cubicle with six roll-aways. Check-in is at eight."

"Cubicle? Check-in at eight?" He viewed me with narrow-eyed suspicion. "Are you sure this isn't a homeless shelter?"

"No, it's a Suckers' Shelter," I confessed. "The roll-aways are $50 each. Did you get the tickets?"

"As Elvis liked to say, I take care of business. There's a Silver ticket for$25 to tour Graceland, a Gold ticket for $40 that includes Graceland and Elvis' Auto & Cycle Museum, and a $50 Platinum ticket that covers Graceland, the Auto Museum, and Elvis' plane - the *Lisa Marie.*"

"You did get the Silver ticket, right?" I asked holding my breath.

"No, no, Little Woman, I splurged on Platinum. Tomorrow, all Elvis, all day."

I should just slit my wrists now, I thought.

The aroma of chlorine stung our nostrils as we entered a lobby with a guitar-shaped pool. Good 'ole boys in blue jeans and their girlfriends in Daisy Dukes were swan-diving off the escalator rails, beer cans in hand as *Don't Be Cruel* blared over the sound system.

"This isn't a pool," George shouted over the din, "it's a huge toilet. The bacterial count must be astronomical. If Elise contracts a flesh-eating disease, her parents will sue our asses off." Elise's parents were attorneys.

His point well-taken, I chirped, "Girls, no swimming just yet."

"Please, please," Lia screamed in my ear, "could we at least put our feet in the water and let the fish bite our toes?"

"There are no fish in swimming pools, Lia," I snapped.

"Yes, there are," she insisted as she dragged me to the edge. "Look at the bottom!"

"Oh, my God," I gasped as I ran over to my husband who stood mesmerized by the Fellini-like scene. "You are not going to believe this. There is shit in the pool."

"Really," he said, "I'm shocked."

A bellboy with a bullhorn bellowed, "Edwards' room ready!"

"Oh, great," George said, "Jist win I was goin' ta order martinis fer the kids and let them chill by the toxic latrine."

Up the escalator and into the third floor banquet room, we found our cubicle with six cots, each covered with a white tablecloth, and the banquet room's refrigerator.

"I've never stayed in a hotel before, Mrs. Edwards," Amy announced. "Why is there such a big refrigerator in our room?"

"That's where you buy food," Gianna, who'd gotten us into this train wreck, explained. "It's filled with little bottles of whiskey and bags of peanuts."

Suddenly I realized we hadn't had dinner and it was ten o'clock. Since the buffet binge, the kids had only had more sugar - candy bars, ice cream and gallons of Slushees. George volunteered to get some hamburgers. He returned with $20 worth of vending machine junk food.

"You're not going to believe this, but if I go out, I can't get back in. They lock the hotel doors at 10 to keep the riff-raff out."

"Mr. Edwards," Elise, the future mini-litigator piped up, "tell them we demand to get our suitcases so we can put on our pajamas."

"Oh, no this will be more fun," I whispered, "We're going to eat Doritos and Twizzlers and then sleep in our clothes!"

"Yippeee," Elise shouted. "When I tell my Mom and Dad what we did on this vacation they're not going to believe it!"

"After Elise's parents finish with us, we'll lose our kids to the Department of Children and Family Services," George commented, "and I'm not going to appeal."

"Let's try to get some sleep," I said, confident he'd relent and after a few months, challenge the court's decision.

At six George announced it was time to rise and shine. No tooth-brushing, no showering - no dressing, for that matter, just breakfast and head over to Graceland. Arriving at eight, we found a huge crowd ahead of us.

"Probably everyone comes here first," my husband figured. "Let's start at the airplane instead."

After an hour and a half in the plane line, we entered the cockpit of the *Lisa Marie,* Elvis' beloved jet named after his only child. He must have decorated the plane about the time his drug use was spinning out of control. Only an hallucinogenic could have prompted 24 karat gold-flecked sinks and gold-plated seat belts. WARNING-DO NOT TOUCH! signs were plastered everywhere. Suddenly alarms and bells were going off and security was rushing the plane as though a sniper was holed up in the fur-walled bathroom. Lia was not in sight. Sure enough, she had jumped on Elvis' bed. Within minutes, we were escorted off the *Lisa Marie.* Being kicked off the plane suited me just fine.

We stood in line for only an hour at the Graceland Auto Museum to view the Pink Cadillac, Ferrari, John Deere tractor and Harley. This time the temptation proved to be too much for Gianna who climbed onto the King's Harley when our backs were turned and, again, Elvis' security force promptly took care of business. We were back in the broiling sun before we'd even seen Elvis's tractor.

Sensing I was near meltdown, George suggested a bit of shopping while he stood guard over our little terrorists outside. I ducked into the Elvis Store where I found a colossal supply of ashtrays, lamps, guitars, lawn mowers, teddy bears, teapots, brassieres - all with The Great One's Coat of Arms, a lightning bolt. The only thing not on display was a replica of the toilet seat he was sitting on the night he fell off the stool and died on the bathroom floor.

As I exited the store, I found Gianna wailing - she wanted to buy an Elvis guitar, Elise pouting - she needed an Elvis wig - and the other two arguing.

"I think they're hungry," my husband said. "Let's go to the Elvis Café."

They ordered Elvis' favorite - a deep-fried sandwich of bananas, peanut butter and marshmallow fluff with a side of French fries and a deep-fried pickle. The big girls shared a piece of Sweet Potato Cream Cheese Pie. Lia and Elise had Moon Pies.

We waddled over to Graceland where the line of mutants from another planet snaked around the block - 75 year-old ingénues with lightning bolts tattooed on their breasts, dudes in high heels and make-up, a man in SCUBA diving gear and a lady with a raccoon on a leash to name but a few. Taking up the rear, Lia threw the mother of all tantrums-"I hate Elvis! This is the dumbest vacation I ever went on in my life! This is all Gianna's fault! I am sick of Elvis and his stupid songs

"Calm her down," George hissed. "People are staring."

"Staring? *At us*?" I hissed. "They're staring *at us*?"

"Mom," Lia, having tantrumed out, called to me, "what does 'Elvis sucks elephant dick' mean?" I spun around to read the graffiti that completely covered the five-foot stone wall surrounding America's second most visited historic residence after The White House. Amy ran over with an eye-witness report. "Mrs. Edwards, a guy dressed like Elvis just peed on the wall to clean off a space so he could write something." "Amy, maybe it was Elvis peeing," Gianna suggested. "That lady over there in the nightgown told me Elvis is not dead."

I could not fathom what I'd done in a past life to deserve this. *Would our country make it to the new millennium,* I wondered, *and, more importantly, did we deserve to?*

At last we entered the hallowed Graceland.

Saddam Hussein had nothing on Elvis in the home decor arena. The "jungle" den, the billiards room, the TV room where Elvis shot out the screen once when he didn't like the program, the gun room where he practiced target shooting, past his parents' bedroom, into the kitchen where he'd made his heart-attack-on-a-plate snacks - we saw it all. We ogled his trophies, Gold Records, jewelry, costumes and awards. The only significant sacred site we did not see was the infamous bathroom.

The tour ended in the Meditation Garden where speakers, hidden under bushes, blared *How Great Thou Art*. A bit to the left of the swimming pool, flanked by the tombs of his parents, Vernon and Gladys, Elvis rests.

His autopsy revealed he'd ingested at least 10 different drugs, including morphine, within the last 24 hours of his life.

How many drugs, I wonder, would Elvis have taken if he'd known Michael Jackson would one day be his son-in-law?

LESSONS LEARNED

. . . people will forget what you said, people will forget what you did, but people will never forget how you made them feel."

~ Maya Angelou ~

THE GREATEST OF THESE

Ellie Searl

The just-married couple embraced, kissed softly, and held onto each other, a little longer than usual, it seemed, as though they couldn't let go for fear it might all just fade away like a slow-moving sun as it slithers below the horizon.

I took pictures of the crowd, and of the lanterns, and of the flowers, and of the tasseled wedding program resting on the seat of a white chair, and of the radiance streaming through the branches.

My husband, Ed, a Unitarian Universalist minister, often asks me to go with him when he officiates at a wedding for people I don't know. He gives me compelling reasons to attend, probably because he doesn't like to go alone: the mother is a famous writer, the father is a New Delhi cartoonist, the bride is an Argentinean swimmer, the groom is a relative of Andrew Wyeth, the reception will be at the Newberry Library. "It will be great fun." He says. "You'll love it."

So when Ed asked, "Want to go to a wedding in Dubuque? It's in a park overlooking the Mississippi, and the reception is at Eagle Ridge Resort. Should be pretty,"

I thought - *Road trip. Wedding in Iowa. Reception in Galena. Yes.*

And when he told me who was getting married - *Absolutely.* This was an event I wanted to honor and celebrate, and it didn't matter that I wouldn't know a soul.

It took an hour to drive beyond Chicago suburban strip malls, parking lots, and repetitive housing, into any scenery worth admiring. Pumpkin stands, white-fenced horse farms, grazing Herefords, and endless fields of drying corn stalks released the city knots from my brain. No radio, no cell phone. Just the serenity of sweeping glacier remnants - a perfect blend of smooth, black dirt for harvesting, ponds for fishing, and hills for tobogganing. Glorious.

The wedding was to be held in Iowa's famed Eagle Point Park, overlooking the grandeur and gentle flow of the Mississippi River. The road meandered up and around and up and around the park, past limestone and wood Depression-Era WPA pavilions scattered among maples and elms, oaks and sycamores, to the highest point where the ceremony would take place.

The cloud-cover and damp air during the late afternoon rehearsal kept people huddled in jackets and shawls. Rain was predicted, and I worried that the outdoor wedding the next day would be a bust, people cold and barely protected under the roof of the open pavilion. I looked over the available space and tried to image a hundred white folding chairs squeezed together on the cement square. Anyone seated on the edges would be caught in the rain. I kicked at dead leaves and spider webs and wondered if someone would sweep all this away before 4:00 pm the next day.

Tree branches, sensing the inevitable fall chill, held tightly to their amber leaves, knowing frost would toss the leaves to the ground, where they'd lie in wait for the winter freeze and ultimately be buried in snow. That sense of tenuous security permeated the atmosphere and unsettled the thoughts of family and friends who supported the almost-newlyweds and wished them well, but who didn't know whether to be optimistic or pessimistic for the couple's future.

Sean and Greg had been in a committed relationship for several years, and they were ready to solidify their union with a civil and spiritual ceremony. But there was a major hang-up. It wasn't legal in Illinois where Sean grew up. Then once married, if the couple wanted to live and work in the United States, Greg, a native Australian, would have to procure an American Visa with means other than through his marriage to Sean. Because the US federal government didn't recognize gay marriages.

This devoted couple, who delighted in each other, who intended to spend the entirety of their lives together, and who wanted to have jobs, buy a house, pay taxes, contribute to society, be legally responsible for each other, and live peaceably among other peace-loving people, couldn't do so as a married couple in most states due to laws governing - actually stifling - the lives and activities of same-sex partners. There were only a few states that allowed gays and lesbians to be lawfully married, complete with the constitutional rights that accompanied the union. Iowa was one of them.

I thought about my Uncle Charlie and his partner Jack, who for so many years hid their love for each other under a barrel called "friends who travel together." Uncle Charlie and Jack stayed in a strong, committed relationship until Charlie died after a long illness at 83. I adored Charlie and Jack. I loved their visits to our house when I was a kid. They made me feel important. Jack read stories to me and played the piano while I sang. Charlie and Jack listened to me yammer on and on, never once shooing me away. They paid more attention to me than my parents did. They admired me, they treated me with respect, and they helped me build my confidence.

It wasn't until I was in high school that I figured out their relationship, and then I wondered why my mother, who certainly knew, made them sleep in separate bedrooms.

Eventually Jack adopted Charlie as his son. That was the only way Jack could legally make medical decisions when Charlie was hospitalized. It was all so secret. All so cautious. And all so sad. My dear uncle and his beloved Jack had to keep their relationship clandestine because same-sex relationships were illegal - judged vulgar, depraved, a corruption of human nature. Something to ridicule.

If only Charlie and Jack could have been with me at the park, witnessing the excited, playful antics of Sean and Greg as they and the wedding party rehearsed with Ed, while family and invited friends clapped and whooped in the background. I wanted Charlie and Jack to see that attitudes in our country had slowly changed over the years – that some states respected same-sex commitments and even offered them legal status. It was too late for my uncle and Jack to have a marriage recorded in the archives of any state history, but it wasn't too late for Sean and Greg.

Sean's mother, Jackie, asked me to take extra pictures of the rehearsal and wedding, so I accommodated my desire to have my own set of photos as well as her need to document her son's celebration. There was something particularly special about this wedding, this couple, this family, this venue – and I wanted photos for me so I could memorialize the event, not merely through personal recollection, which could alter truth and feeling, but with tangible images that captured the love and beauty of this short, yet momentous, slice of Sean and Greg's journey to happiness. Perhaps I also wanted an homage to Charlie and Jack.

Ed was great at the rehearsal. He helped the wedding party find comfort levels within the anxiety that ran rampant among them. The couple was anxious about the huge commitment they were making, and they worried they'd falter when they said the vows they had written. Those standing up for the couple worried they'd mess up their parts and spoil everything. And they *all* worried about the reactions of naysayers and skeptics who still didn't support this, nor any other, gay marriage.

Ed calmly directed everyone through the processional, the readings, the pronouncements, and the recessional. He reminded them that, yes, this was serious business, but it was a joyous occasion; it should be fun. He cracked jokes. They laughed and relaxed.

Sean's sister, Maureen, practiced her reading from 1 Corinthians Chapter 13. She figured that if she read it ahead of time, she wouldn't cry during the ceremony. "Love bears all things, believes all things, hopes all things, endures all things. Love never ends. So faith, hope, love abide – these three. But the greatest of these is love."

She turned to Ed. "Is it ok if I hug Sean and Greg after I read that?" And everyone laughed again.

There is always the moment at the conclusion of a wedding when the minister presents the couple to those gathered. Ed makes sure it what the couple wants. Most times it's the traditional ". . . George and Mary,

Husband and Wife." Infrequently it's the outdated, patriarchal, ". . . Mr. and Mrs. Walters," Sometimes it's simply, ". . . the Newlyweds."

"So how are we going to announce you two? Do you want me to say, 'I now present Greg and Sean, Spouses? Mr. and Mr.? Newly Wedded Men?"

Someone offered, "How about Husband and Husband?" And it was settled.

Rehearsal dinners can be awkward, with people seated at long tables in a restaurant's back room, where conversation is difficult and food is passed family style, the big eaters taking the best pieces of chicken before it reaches the last person. But Jackie and her husband Dan hosted their rehearsal dinner with charm and grace at The Irish Cottage in historic Galena. No sit-down dinner. Instead, a lovely array of entrée hors d'oeuvres - displayed buffet style, with beer, wine, and cocktails - all in the comfort of a private living room. Just like home.

We sat on couches and over-stuffed chairs and drank champagne and ate cocoanut shrimp and chatted about whether or not it would rain at the wedding, and when the couple would return to London so Sean could finish Veterinary school, and how it was too expensive for Greg's family to travel all the way from Australia for the wedding, so there would be a celebration in his hometown later on in the year, and that Greg, a baker by trade, was going to take courses in a career that was needed in the United States so he could apply for an American work visa.

Then we all went to the bar and watched Irish dancers toe-tap their way through precision routines.

It was when I showed Sean's dad the rehearsal pictures that I understood the full significance of this wedding and his deep gratitude for all the support and encouragement extended to Sean and Greg.

Dan's eyes filled with tears, and he talked about being a father. "I have only ever wanted health and happiness for my son. He was ill for many years as a teenager, and he lost out on what most kids take for granted. Now he's well and deeply in love. It is gratifying that he found his true path - that he found Greg - and that Greg makes him so happy. I am beyond grateful." Dan lowered his head and wiped his eyes.

What does one say after a such a deep-felt declaration of the heart? "You're right?" "I agree?" "I know what you feel?" No. It wasn't about right – or wrong. It didn't matter if I agreed – or not. And how could I possibly know what he, Sean's father, felt after twenty-some years of hoping his son would find his rightful place in a world where overly-traditional people were still too ready and willing to denigrate those with differences, whether related to race, gender, age, religion, politics, or sexual preference. I hadn't experienced that. I hadn't experienced a callous populace unsympathetic to, nor intolerant of, the direction my child had taken in life.

I said, "Sean and Greg are fortunate to have each other. Sean is especially fortunate to have you and Jackie as parents. He grew up in a loving, accepting household. Ours would be a better country if we could say that about everyone."

Dan thanked me, smiled, and clinked my glass. "Here's to Husband and Husband." Then someone grabbed Dan's arm and dragged him into the bar to watch the Irish dancers. I laughed and thought about how much I loved my life right then.

The day of the wedding changed from overcast to slightly sunny to magnificent, rather like a bad mood that realizes it's more pleasant, and even easier, to laugh off whatever is making the nerves ache. Guests assembled at the pavilion, and although there were a few people unable to sanction the soon-to-take-place same-sex marriage, they were there, in attendance - with gifts, which spoke louder, and held more importance, than any private opinion about holy matrimony and its traditions.

"Family and friends, I present to you, Sean and Greg, Husband and Husband." Everyone clapped as the musicians played the first notes of the recessional.

Sunlight streamed through the golden tree-gazebo, creating a wispy glow, like a luminous blush under a billow of sheer fabric as it floats in slow motion to the ground. The halo-effect hovered over Sean and Greg touching them like a blessing as they held hands and walked down the aisle, through the leaves, into their lives together.

NOT GOOD ENOUGH

Mary Lou Edwards

"Who do you think you are? You're not a movie star. This is good enough for you."

My dentist, Dr. Z., was talking down into my open mouth. I was 14 and sat in the chair, paralyzed in position and perplexed. I wasn't angry, just baffled. When my tooth cracked while chewing a Lemonhead, I dreaded my fate - needles and drills were not my idea of fun - but now, after I'd endured 10 agonizing visits, I was feeling a different sort of pain, a kind of slap-in-the-face pain.

"What are you talking about?" I asked hulking Dr. Z. whose giant head was in my face. "You don't know if I'll grow up to be a movie star." I didn't think I wanted to be in movies, but my mom told me I could be whatever I wanted after I finished my education so maybe I would decide to be like Audrey Hepburn. "You don't know what I'm going to be," I blurted, saliva dripping down the side of my still anesthetized mouth. "And why is this good enough for me?" Despite my fear of Dr. Z telling my father I was argumentative, I could not help questioning this ridiculous excuse for a repair job.

I took another look at the horrible tooth in the hand-held mirror. "This looks OK for a temporary fix, but I don't want this tooth forever."

"If you don't like it, don't come back," he yelled; then he yanked the little round mirror out of my hand. "No little snip is going to come in here and teach me dentistry."

Little Snot! Now I was angry. I didn't even care if he told my dad.

"You said you'd fix my tooth," I said as I struggled out of the dental chair. "Don't yell at me because you didn't do it right. This doesn't even look like a tooth - this looks like you painted a tiny piece of Tootsie-Roll white and glued it in my mouth. And don't worry about me coming back," I added, as I ran out the door, "I wouldn't come back if my teeth fell out!"

I cried all the way home - partly because I was going to be in big trouble with my dad who thought Dr. Z was a big deal because he had a college degree, and partly because my tooth looked like a pencil eraser.

When I ran into my house, I found my mother at the stove boiling water for macaroni. I didn't want to bother her because supper had to be on the table at 4:30 sharp or my father would . . . actually I didn't know what my father would do if dinner wasn't on the table because my mother was never a minute late. No one wanted to irritate a man whose tantrums were legendary. Sometimes his rages were pretty funny - a grown person acting like a spoiled brat - sometimes I'd aggravate him just to see him throw a fit. But I did not want to risk him boiling over like Mt. Vesuvius if supper wasn't on time so I just sat at the table sniveling.

"You're home early. Why are you crying," my mom asked as she stirred the pot of gravy. "Didn't the dentist give you Novocain?"

"You won't believe my snaggle-tooth," I sobbed, hardly able to catch my breath. "I'm never going out again as long as I live."

"Oh, stop it. You're going to give yourself hiccups - let me see the tooth." She squeezed my chin and forced my mouth to open wide. "Well," she said after the inspection, at least it's not in the front. You're lucky, you can hardly see it."

"See," I wailed, "even you think it's bad. You can see it when I smile big. I'll have to talk like a ventriloquist."

"Don't be ridiculous. The rest of your teeth are perfect. Are you going to let one little nub put in by an incompetent upset you?"

I was about to start raving about her calling it *a nub, a nub, my own mother calling it a nub*, but I stopped in amazement. "Did you call Dr. Z incompetent?" I asked.

I knew she didn't much care for Dr. Z.   Once I overheard her say to my father, "Jim, the man is so high and mighty he looks down on people. He puts his pants on one leg at a time like everyone else," but she'd never say that in front of us kids.

"Momma, he is incompetent. I told him my tooth looked like a bitsy stub, and he yelled that I shouldn't come back which is fine with me. I hate the guy."

"Watch your mouth," she warned. "Hate is not a nice word."

"OK, then I can't stand him. He told me I'm not so important that I need a perfect tooth. He said this tooth is good enough for you."

Hearing that, my mother, who had been hustling to make that 4:30 deadline, spun around from the kitchen sink. I didn't know if the steam was coming from the pot of pasta she was draining into the colander or if it was coming from her head.

"He said what?" she snapped.

"You heard me. He said this botched up tooth is good enough for me."

"Well that bastard," she blurted. My eyes popped open like one of those push-button umbrellas. My mother never swore. Sometimes she said heck or darn, maybe dammit if she was really ticked, but bastard? Never, ever. I was shocked. And then, she said it again. "That bastard!"

only this time she said it under her breath and with a slow, deliberate enunciation as though I wasn't even there in front of her, as though she was looking at a picture only she could see.

"Sit down, Honey, and quit whining about that tooth. We'll get it fixed right," she promised, "but what that bastard said is far more important."

Whoa, that was the third time she swore. Was she forgetting that God was listening and she'd be punished? Getting a little nervous - about God, about 4:30 - I said, "Mom, you'd better finish cooking."

"Don't worry about dinner. This is more important," she said, tapping her finger on the kitchen table.

Was she kidding - more important than my dad walking through the door at suppertime? This was incredible - this I had to hear.

"Never let anyone tell you who you are or what you're worth," she seethed. "Never believe anyone who says you're not important - that good enough is good enough for you. That arrogant bastard!"

Four times. That was the fourth time! She is playing with fire," I thought, but there was no stopping her.

"That arrogant bastard thinks he can look down on people because he has a couple of capital letters after his name - that he's better than everyone else. He's a poor excuse for a man."

"Mom," I said, "I'm mad, but you're even angrier than I am."

"Mary Lou, when I was growing up I met way too many self-important, cruel bastards."

That's it. Here comes the lightning bolt. My father will come in expecting supper and find us slumped over the table.

"I met bastards who thought it was OK to treat people like dirt. A priest made me stand in the vestibule during Mass because I didn't have a nickel for the collection basket," she said digging out a memory she'd buried long ago. "I went to a grocer who switched a loaf of stale bread for a fresh one, and said, 'I'm saving this loaf for someone else. This one is good enough for your mother." Now she was on a tear. "Years ago epileptics weren't allowed to go to school. My father died in the 1918 flu epidemic, and your Nonna had to work leaving my grandparents to watch my younger brother who suffered seizures. He'd come to my school and stare at me through the window, longing to have a seat in my classroom, wanting to be like the other kids. My teacher said that since my grandparents obviously couldn't handle him, and since he wasn't good enough to come to school, I should just stay home and watch him."

"Mom, stop. You're making me want to cry."

"I'll stop. I have to get dinner. Now set the table," she said noticing the time, "but don't ever forget," she warned wagging a finger in my face, "you are better than no one, and no one is better than you. That bastard had a hell of a lot of nerve."

Bastard - hell - two swear words in one sentence? God must be croaking.

As I put the last fork and knife on the table, my father walked in through the back door.

"What smells so good? How was school?"

"School was fine, but look at my ugly tooth," I said, stretching my mouth so he could get a good look.

"Give Dr. Z time. When he's finished, it'll look good as new - that's only a temporary."

"No, Jim," my mother said, "that's the finished product. He thinks he can foist second-rate work on peons. That goof's specialty is pulling teeth. He thinks that's all people in this neighborhood deserve. He's a bastard who thinks he's better than everyone else."

Oh, no, now bastard is going to set my father off. That's almost worse than getting God angry.

"Really, Daddy, it's true. The tooth is finished," I said trying to stem a tirade about my mom saying *bastard*. "I told Dr. Z that I wouldn't call this a tooth, and he said I'm not a movie star - that this tooth is good enough for me."

I could see the tension in my father's jaw, his face simmering with fury. The gravy boiled over, and I thought he would too. I expected him to blast me with - "who do you think you are to talk back to a dentist?" But

I was in for a shock. Dad's temple's veins throbbed like an alarm, and he said -

"He said that to you?" Only he didn't say it like my mother had said it, low and under her breath. He said it in a loud voice, in an ominous voice that meant someone was in trouble. "Really - he said that? Dr. Z told you that? Amazing. Well after supper we'll pay him a little visit."

I knew my dad was going to go over there and have a few words, maybe even a little explosion. But I didn't feel one bit sorry for the bully. He was going to learn that we weren't better than anyone, and no one was better than us. And maybe, Dr. Z was just not good enough to be our dentist.

Up Deep Creek

Carolyn B Healy

I stood on the bank and squinted at the two white-clad figures in the middle of Deep Creek's swirling water. As a nine year-old city girl temporarily plunked down in the Smoky Mountains for a family visit, I was on high alert for things I couldn't see back at home, and this was going to be a big one. My cousin Annette, six years older, was on the list of my most admired people. She could cook and sew and win 4H prizes. She had the same name as my favorite Mouseketeer, and I harbored a secret hunch that she was really the famous Annette and the family was keeping it secret. Plus, she was a teenager with teenage friends, some of them boys.

Now she was standing in the middle of the creek in a pretty white dress with lace trim. I bet she made it, I thought in a spurt of pride. I knew from experience what she was up against out there. That water was cold as ice. I knew that because her mother Anna Lou would regularly pile the cousins into her Plymouth and barrel over mountain roads to take us to the swimming hole "up Deep Creek" and then back to her house for popsicles.

Part of my annual immersion into the ways of my relatives was the agonizing entry into that frigid water, a test I had to pass to prove myself. While my cousins dove in and got it over with, I inched in, crunching down to pat the freezing water onto my goose-bumped arms. Once I finally gathered my courage and plunged in, it was a victory. Annette didn't usually go along, being too busy with more sophisticated endeavors.

I stood on the bank behind Anna Lou and Uncle Commodore, my mother's brother, and their sons Don and Jim. They seemed to think this was a normal occurrence. I had heard we were going to a baptism but that sounded like a churchy thing, not a swimming hole thing. What were we doing here? And what was a baptism anyway?

Was my petite Grandma there, having clambered down the bank on her tender feet, in her voile dress and Sunday hat with the veil? You know how memory is, focusing in on the main event and leaving the edges blurry. Grandma may have stayed home, since this was a Presbyterian ceremony and the rest of the family, she included, was Baptist. I didn't know the difference, but there must have been one.

There was a lot of religion in that town. The various Baptist churches, red brick with white steeples in town and the more modest weathered wooden ones up the hollows, seemed to have the strongest foothold. One recent day, I had tagged along on an all-day genealogy outing up into the mountains with my aunts. I snapped pictures of the white clapboard church that a great-grandfather had built, and of the family headstones that surrounded it. It was something. How could a kid from 111th Street have roots way out here, in a hollow that my aunts could barely find? I was more interesting than I'd thought.

The Presbyterian Church that my cousin was seeking entry to was back in town, painted bright white, right down the hill from her house, a couple of blocks from the almost defunct railroad line, just around the bend from the Baptist one of the rest of the family. But the church that made the biggest impression on me was the one that we had nothing to do with. It announced itself by a gothic-script sign on the highway into town: *St. Joseph Roman Catholic Church, Masses 8, 9, 10:30 am.* It sat on a ridge overlooking the A&P and the Tuckasiegee River, its austere grey stone looking medieval and menacing. I didn't stop to think that my home church back in Chicago was housed in an odd replica limestone Irish castle that must have looked as misplaced as this one. It also escaped me that my Unitarian church building served as the symbol for the South Side neighborhood that was so heavily Catholic it practically smelled of incense. Nine year-olds aren't much on irony.

The ceremony was about to start. The other figure, the white-suited preacher, began to stir. He boomed a few words in his God-calling voice, put his arm around my willing cousin and – oh my gosh – dipped her backwards under the water. And held her there. And kept holding her there. Her family stood stock still. Since they were older than I was and better swimmers, I figured that if she needed rescue, they'd be on the job, and I should quell my impulse to splash out there.

The preacher's incantations continued and to my relief he finally lifted her up, streaming, still breathing, and escorted her to the bank where her mother waited with a white terrycloth towel. We trooped back to the house for the usual pot luck – plates of sliced tomato and cantaloupe still warm from the sun, pyramids of sweet corn picked that morning, fried okra, stacks of cornbread, beef cooked beyond well-done to just this side of charcoalhood, and fried chicken from the poor creature I'd seen my grandfather ax-murder earlier in the day. I might have been the one from the city, but in their way, my relatives were far more conversant with violence than I was, but the necessary violence it takes to run a life close to the land. Dessert was Anna Lou's coconut cake and watermelon, eaten in the yard so the juice could run down to the elbows.

I never asked Annette what it felt like to be dunked and baptized, being too shy and too young. I didn't yet know that the result of curiosity could be learning, if only I'd ask. I remember how it felt to me. I'd glimpsed a jaw-dropping event I'd never see again and that my friends back home couldn't imagine. For a while, the gulf between me and my relatives had widened, with me on the outside peeking in, wondering what would happen next.

But by the end of the meal, while the aunts cleared the table and teased Grandma into sitting on the convertible step-stool while they washed the dishes, and the men rocked on the porch, I played with my cousins out by the lilac bush. We chased fireflies and captured them in Ball jars with perforated lids that stayed on the back porch. Laughter leaked out of the kitchen windows, and the low rumble of the uncles' voices rolled off the porch. In the process, I was restored. This was my family. I loved their slow speech and Southern story-telling. I loved their food, and how they loved my mother. And I loved Annette who gave me something to shoot for.

I wasn't required to understand all their ways to belong there. It was a great gift of my childhood to see so early that we could be different yet connected. Annette was the star of that day in my memory but I think I was the lucky one. Later, dishes done, we all gathered in the front room and sat in a giant circle, moths hitting the screens, and the funny stories began. What I would give for a chance to hear those voices again, trying to top each other. Their generation is all gone now except for Commodore who celebrated his 100th birthday this summer. I inhaled all that love and knew I'd have a home here if I ever needed it, and vowed to take all these folks home with me in my memory, where they still reside.

FRIENDSHIP

A friend is someone who is there for you
when he'd rather be anywhere else

~ Len Wei ~

CRASH COURSE

Mary Lou Edwards

Where did I come from—how did I get here? No one agreed.

My brother said "the stork brought me."

My girlfriend said "fairies delivered babies."

The girl upstairs said "babies were left on doorsteps."

My cousin told me doctors carried dead babies in their black bags and a mother gives life by breathing into the baby's nose. Raphaella (Raphy)

Saridiso, my fifth-grade best friend forever, told me she saw some weird looking babies in glass jars at the Museum of Science and Industry.

"Raphy," I said, "that is so stupid. Babies do not come in glass jars."

"Well, I went to the Museum's Chick Hatchery, and I saw with my own eyes baby chickens pop out of eggs. If a chick can crack out of an egg, why can't a baby come packed in a jar?" she reasoned.

Maybe she's right I thought. Everyone says I look like my dad. Maybe my mother picked my jar because I had eyes that reminded her of my father.

"That makes sense, Raphy, but you're forgetting one thing. Mothers get babies from hospitals not museums," I said with more than a bit of scorn.

"Not always," Raphaella countered, "you heard Sister Praxeda tell the Christmas story about the stable, and you saw the eighth graders' Nativity play. Jesus was packed in straw. They didn't show how he got in the manger in the first place."

"None of this makes sense," I admitted. "They say Mary and Joseph left Nazareth on a donkey and she was great with child. I think they meant she was great with children."

"Oh, I don't believe a lot of things about Christmas," Raphy said, "ever since I found out Santa Claus was a fake, that he didn't fly over houses or come down chimneys, that it was all a big fat lie."

"OK, so Santa's not real, but you're not saying Jesus was a fake too, are you?" I asked aghast.

"Of course not," she reassured me, "but I do wonder what exactly they're talking about when I hear the Christmas story. For instance, what's a Virgin? Was Joseph the father or wasn't he? What the heck are swaddling clothes? And you know what else?" she said stopping to catch her breath, "I think the Three Kings, The Magi, and the Wise Guys are all the same people."

"They are the same, and they're Wise Men not Wise Guys, though I don't know how wise they were bringing frankincense and myrrh to a baby instead of a toy. But why," I asked in exasperation, "are we talking about presents and Santa? We need to find out how kids are born, and we're not even supposed to be talking about this."

"I know," Raphaella lamented. "My mother said I should always come to her if I have any questions, but when I asked where babies came from, she freaked out. She said, 'I'll tell you when you need to know. I'll tell you when the time is right.' In my house, that means never."

I was too embarrassed to tell Raphy how asking about babies almost got me killed.

Once during a family drive, my mother mentioned to my dad that a cousin was "expecting."

Piping up from the backseat, I asked, "When is she due?" I was about eight years old and had no idea what that meant, but I'd heard a neighbor ask that of a pregnant lady, and I thought it sounded grown-up.

"When is she due?" my father shouted as he practically ran our car off the road and screeched to a halt. "Mary," he thundered, "what are you teaching this kid? Where did she learn that? Who is she talking to," he continued bellowing. "You're not watching her friends," he accused. "You need to talk to her teachers! This kid is out of control."

The virulent tongue-lashing almost had my mother in tears and, cowering in the backseat, I vowed never, ever to get my mother in such trouble again, and I never did. Thanks to fear and shame, I remained ignorant for a very long time.

When I became a mother, I vowed no question would go unanswered and no subject would be off limits.

One day, when my daughter was about seven, I found her and her friend, Cara, playing with their beloved Barbies. There were about a dozen of the stupid strumpets swimming in the Barbie pool with a few boyfriend Kens floating around too. One doll caught my eye.

"Lia," I asked, "what's with Ken's head on Barbie's body?"

"Oh, that's Barbie's gay friend," she chirped. "They're going for a swim before they go shopping."

I swear I heard a car crash.

FRIENDS, NOT ENEMIES

Carolyn B Healy

We flew in from the west over O'Hare, then banked over the Loop, studying first the close-together highrises and then the suburban houses ringed with still-green grass. Our friends sat in the row behind us and we talked about how great the city looked if only those puffy white clouds would get out of the way. We'd had a great week playing golf and seeing the Texas Hill Country but it was time to return to normal. We headed for that lovely moment of touchdown, when you are back home where you belong, but not yet overtaken by daily responsibilities. My calendar for the coming week was full. I'd see my writer friends on Tuesday, my poet friend Wednesday, a counselor friend late in the week. I felt fortunate to have all that to return to.

I'd been afraid that the leaves of precious fall, my favorite season, would all be down by the time I got back, a fear that my friend behind me, a dedicated gardener, echoed. But there they were in gorgeous yellows and oranges and reds, hanging onto the branches for all they were worth until we could get home and witness their departure firsthand.

It grew dark as we rode home in the taxi. Once we turned down our street and saw groups of trick-or-treaters and their lurking parents, some dressed up themselves, we realized we were in trouble. It was Halloween and if we stayed home candyless, we would have to hide in the basement until late in the evening. We threw our suitcases in the garage, checked for messages, even though there are few these days since email has replaced the telephone as the delivery method of choice for our friendships. We hopped in the car and went to our favorite bar for dinner and refuge.

Back home later, it was a smooth re-entry. We kept the outside lights off against Halloween stragglers and I threw myself into clothes sorting, old movie-watching and email catching-up. I slept like a baby, exhausted by all the relaxation, the eight-hour sleeps and languorous dreams of a vacation.

In the morning I woke up to a thud, and then another, and another. Sunshine streamed in through my tree-high bedroom window. I saw immediately that I had lost leaves after all. Every one of the bright yellow ones that had graced the tree right outside my window had fallen into a sad pool below, leaving small red berries visible against the bright blue sky. I remembered the benefit of this annual loss - you can see so much better once the leaves come down. I discovered a birds' nest at the crook of two branches that I'd missed in my daily first gaze outside all spring and summer. Had I missed eggs and baby birds too?

Before I even got to the window I figured out the thuds. Dozens of birds swarmed the tree, nipping off berries. Robins, cardinals, finches and sparrows hopped, swooped and kept out of each others' way, feasting like there was no tomorrow. It was a colorful diversity of birds, each with their own ways but all wanting the same thing - those berries. Some of the birds - drunk on fermenting berries? - lost their way and slammed themselves into my windows. I hoped they'd sober up before starting that migration, so they could tell my window from the open sky.

I grabbed my camera and tried to capture them in all their chaotic glory, but they didn't cooperate – too much jumping around. So I settled for the better option, actually watching them. Because we like to see nature as human-centric, it was tempting to think of them as friends enjoying the feast together as we would, like bird Thanksgiving. But with brains smaller than jelly beans, they can't manage that. They don't have room for mirror neurons and consciousness and the desire to be understood, the fundamentals of friendship. They just chowed down and leapt from one branch to the other, doing their different dances.

I'm pretty interested in sorting out differences. As a therapist, I've always had to search through the surface differences among my clients to find the shared core of emotion and motivation and vision that allows for change. And as a writer I am taken with point of view, always imagining how various characters would see the same event so differently. In fact, if I don't look out, I can get so wrapped up in examining everyone's unique take that I forget to tell the story, or take so long that everybody including me has lost interest. Focus, I am learning, is a necessary antidote to this overload of empathy.

As a morning birdwatcher, I studied how each species looked different as they got the same job done. Years ago when I first started to learn a bit about brain science, one portion of the brain was credited with the ability to discern small details, like telling one species of bird from another. The next time I tuned in, the same part of the brain was described as the place where face recognition took place, and I heard the sad tale of a man who had lost that ability. As he walked down the street, he had no way to know if he was encountering his best friend or a complete stranger because he couldn't sort out one face from another. Much embarrassment ensued as he struggled to manage this deficit. He truly couldn't tell who his friends were until he heard their voices.

As a friend, I am watchful for differences too. I have friends of many stripes. Differences in politics, religion, life circumstance, ethnic heritage, whatever, do not stop me. Being just like me isn't nearly as important as being interesting and willing to share. This does not make me a good person, just a curious one.

I know that not everyone sees it this way. A long conversation with a friend last spring revealed that she does not have any friends who disagree with her, and likes it that way. I began to mention that conversation to other friends and found several more who said the same. During the political season I heard a similar tale from many more. They choose a cocoon of commonality and self-affirmation, secure in their beliefs together.

That's a lot of comfort, but at what cost? In my experience, sad to say, people who stick to their own kind can become a little superior, and smug, and self-righteous if they encounter nothing but agreement. Do I sound like a scold? My question is this: How do you grow and change and enlarge your view inside such insulation? What challenges you to rethink and fine-tune what you believe if you never test it against others' thoughts and feelings?

My argument in favor of cultivating friendships with those who have differing views is this: If you hear an unfamiliar viewpoint from a person you know and trust, chances are you will consider it because you care about what matters to your friend. And you may even deepen your understanding of the issue by seeing it from another vantage point.

It is quite another thing if the only varying views you consider are the top-of-the-lungs rants of media pundits who get rich on the numbers of listeners they can recruit to their side. They trade on fear of The Other, and exaggerate the threat of other ideas, attributing evil motives to those who disagree.   Predicting catastrophe is big business out there, and works to increase suspicion and split people apart, the opposite of friendship.

The one ingredient that is present in friendship and absent just about everywhere else these days is respect. If my friend tells me a story of her dilemma years ago as a young coed, knowing that a classmate was about to have an abortion which she felt was "just about the worst thing," and shares with me the helpful counsel of a nun she consulted, I can understand something new and appreciate how she was tested by that experience.

If my friend tells me that he would love to speak out on human rights abuses in his homeland but can't afford to place his family in jeopardy, I gain a deeper understanding of what is at stake there and how grateful I should be for what we have here.

If I hear from my friend about a long ago summer when his all-white community turned into a nearly all-black community almost overnight, leaving his parents feeling that they had to upend the family and disrupt their comfortable lives, I am left to appreciate the work he had to do to overcome bitterness and resentment for what they lost.

Sure, there are awkward moments when I bite my tongue, and times when I don't, and the endless internal debate about when to do each. And, like everyone else, I savor the times I can relax from that stress and hang out with people who largely agree with me.

As a young person I used to think I was 100% right all the time, which surely made me a real pain in the ass to people I disagreed with. Now I don't think I'm so right. I aspire be right for me today, and I'll try again tomorrow as I keep being challenged to consider new ideas.

The biggest change I've seen with my maturity is that now I've become a pain in the ass to the people I basically agree with, peppering them with comments like Wait a minute or Did you think about this or Here's what my friend told me.

If respect is in place, we can tread that middle ground just fine. If not, if one person seeks to overpower and convert the other, the gulf widens. As I saw from the plane, it's a beautiful world we live in. And as I observed about all those birds, if we can work around each other harmoniously we can all get what we want. And as I see my friends this week, I'll find I have a lot to learn.

SMALL (TOWN) FRIENDS

Ellie Searl

Before Becky moved to town, Gloria was supposedly my best friend, although I never much liked her. She was mean. And bossy. At her house, we played her games, danced her way, and ate her peanut butter, potato chip, cream cheese, and pickle sandwich creations. At my house, she rode my bike, used my mother's lipstick, and dulled the tops of my new crayons.   But she seemed popular with the other kids, so by association, I was popular too.   I didn't understand enough about personality types to figure that because she bullied her way into relationships, probably everybody hated her.

My friendship with Gloria rounded a nasty corner in 5th grade, a month before her soon-to-be-mirror-image arrived.   It was at Christmas time, when schools actually celebrated Christmas, before public institutions had to recognize the separation of church and state.

Our school had a tradition of painting scenes on classroom windows for the holidays.   On Halloween, we not only painted scenes on the school windows, but we also took a field trip into the village with all of our paraphernalia and painted our designs across huge store windows - Jack-o-lanterns, and witches with black cats riding on broom sticks across a crescent moon, ghosts wafting over scarecrows sitting in dried-up cornfields - all the while keeping balance on ladders propped up against thick panes of glass.   My parents owned the general store in the center of town, so it was a special treat if I painted those windows.   But the big kids usually got there first, pushing and shoving their way to the front of the bus; then racing to the best windows when we arrived.

This particular Christmas, our teacher announced a contest - four students would win the honor of painting a scene on the classroom windows.   And not only that, the winners would go into town and paint Christmas on all the storefronts.   To be considered, we were to submit a hand-drawn picture of Santa.   The rules were simple: draw the picture at home, have no help from adults, and do not trace.   *This was a cinch,* I thought.   I was good at drawing pictures, so I knew I'd win.   There were a few times when solid confidence led my way, and this was one of them.

In the Saturday Evening Post that afternoon, I found a small black and white sketch of a smiling Santa, a bag stuffed with toys slung over his shoulder.   He stood ankle-deep in a pile of wrapped gifts, boot-fur peeking over the bows and ribbons.   This was it.

I had a good eye - a natural instinct for proportion and the elements of detail.   With a sharpened pencil and oversized sketchpad, I drew a likeness of the picture, making it much bigger, and Santa much paunchier, than what was represented in the Post.   No, I didn't trace it; that would have been cheating.   But Miss Cuomo never said we couldn't *look* at a picture and make one like it. She never said it had to be *straight* from our imaginations. I submitted my big Santa to her the next morning.

Most of the other kids in the class didn't bother to enter the contest. They already knew they weren't good enough and wouldn't win, their levels of artistic confidence much lower than mine. Miss Cuomo said my picture was the best, and she gave me the window that overlooked the playground and parking lot where everyone could see it. Was I proud! And I'd be going into the village the next day with the other winners. I'd get to paint the front window of my parents' general store.

I gathered my colors, hopped up onto window ledge, and started my painting. The non-winners watched with envy, and the non-participators colored mimeographed pictures of Santa's Workshop.

Within five minutes, Miss Cuomo called, "Eloise, come here."

I turned around, holding a long, thin paintbrush in mid-air and looked at her, not sure I had heard correctly. A splot of red paint dropped onto the toe of my Mary Janes.

"Eloise. Come down from there."

I stuck the paintbrush into the tin can and hopped down. The hem of my dress caught on the long handle and knocked the can to the floor. Red paint oozed out, spreading a blood-pool across the linoleum.

Miss Cuomo bent over to rescue the brush and can. She looked up at me from the floor. "Did you draw that Santa yourself?" She walked to the counter and heaved the dripping supplies into the sink. She jerked around, giving me one of those stern teacher glares, and slapped her hands on her hips. "Did you?" she barked.

"Yes, Miss Cuomo," I stammered. "I drew it. . .. myself . . . yesterday . . . after school. Ask my mom."

"Gloria said you traced it."

I looked over at Gloria standing at her desk, arms folded, grinning. Her snarl said, *You're a pig. My picture wasn't picked, so I'm going to make sure you can't paint either.*

I stifled the urge to leap across the room and wring her neck. Hate isn't a strong enough word to describe how I felt about her right then.

My throat tightened. "I didn't trace it," I cried. "I saw it in a magazine and drew one like it." Tears made my nose tickle. Everyone stared. They probably all thought I cheated.

"Well," Miss Cuomo huffed, "I should have looked at your picture more carefully." She took a breath and continued her attack on the exhale. "Now that I think about it, your picture is really too good for anyone your age to draw. So . . ." She paused. I waited.

When I think back at that pause, I realize she was stuck in a teacher quagmire created by loss of control and a tattletale - *cheating might be running amuck on my watch, which, if I let it continue, will ruin my integrity as an authoritarian forever.* But at the time, I thought she was a mean old hag who believed a brat.

"So . . ." she sighed, ". . . you aren't going to paint anymore." Her voice regained its momentum, strong and loud, as she settled into the finality of her decision. "And you're not going into town tomorrow. Go to your seat. Now."

I was devastated! How could I extricate myself from this humiliating, exceedingly unfair situation? Gloria had lied, but the teacher had spoken with conviction. I was doomed.

Keeping any trace of whine from my voice, I protested one last time. "Gloria lied. I drew it myself. The picture was much smaller. I drew it myself. I did. She lied."

"Enough. Go to your seat. Here - color this." She shoved a wrinkled mimeographed paper into my hand - a purple outlined picture of Santa's elves pounding nails into a doghouse with "Fido" printed on the gabled roof.

I looked at my feet and, through tears, saw red paint trickle from the tip of my shoe into my sock. I'd been stripped of my place of honor, I wouldn't get to paint my mom and dad's store window the next day, I was embarrassed beyond belief, and I would more than likely get in trouble for wrecking the shoes and socks I was only supposed to wear on

Sundays. I sat at my desk, and shook with silent sobs, feeling my faith in humanity go looping round and round a downward spiral.

I sent dagger eyes at Gloria, but by this time she was hiding her face inside her open desk and sniggering, as though she shared some sadistic secret with her scissors and glue. Everyone else was silent, having been stunned into their work with such pretend concentration that only the fire alarm could have raised their heads.

After that episode, my association with Gloria dwindled from friend to acquaintance. She switched her attentions to Becky when she arrived in January, and I took up with Kristen, whose family moved to town a few months later.

For the next few years, Kristen and I carried on as much of a friendship as she could muster, given her predisposition to ignore me whenever someone more important was around. We drank cherry cokes and ate Nabs at the drug store, drooled over pictures of Paul Newman, smoked cigarettes behind the fair grounds, read smutty magazines at the beach, and gossiped about Gloria and Becky.

I felt like a grown-up with Kristen. She had a city sophistication about her and knew the Exclusive Summer People who sailed on their private yachts to Westport from New York City and Washington, DC, and stayed in their lake houses. Besides, meals at Kristen's house were better than Gloria's PB&P&PC&CC sandwiches. Roast beef served at the dining room table on gold placemats, and formal, somewhat stilted conversation with Kristen's librarian mother and doctor father. They treated their guests with respect; although, as represented in Kristen's on-and-off attention, a bit of arrogance mixed in with condescension was present in most of the family gatherings with locals like me.

At the beginning of 9th grade, Kristen was sent to a private boarding school. It was less than a two-hour drive away, but it was on the other side of the Adirondack Mountains, and it seemed like a million miles to me. A couple of days before she left for her first semester as a freshman, she mused about being so far from home for so long. She said, "Don't be surprised if I forget your name. I'm going to meet lots of new friends at school, and I won't have space in my brain for everyone." The funny thing was, I thought this made sense. I didn't get offended until a few years later when I realized how insensitive and particularly stupid her remark.

In our town of 800, most of the kids my age came from farm or logging families and lived way out on unpaved country roads in the foothills - the Rural Route, according to the post office. Their family circumstances didn't allow them much opportunity to socialize - lots of chores and little access to transportation into the village. So, when we were in 9th and 10th grades, before we all started to drive, I had to pal around with kids who lived in the village. Becky, Gloria, and Kristen lived in the village, and Kristen was off learning new names and forgetting mine.

After Kristen left in September, I was stuck with reestablishing a quasi-friendship with Gloria and Becky, who by this time, had morphed into the Doublemint Twins - same sweater sets, same clutch purses, same bouffant hairstyles pinned up with the same sequined barrettes, same sing-songy voices.

Conjoined twins saw less of each other than did Becky and Gloria. Attached at the emotional hip, they didn't go anywhere or do anything without the other – at least not during the day. Their identities must have taken a nosedive when they went home. How did they survive alone with just their families? Did they experience mini-emotional breakdowns? Lose their appetites? Wither away in their rooms? Did their mothers, with sinking feeling and crinkled brow, wonder, "Where did my cheery little girl go?" Did they stare at, but pay no attention to, gorgeous David Considine saunter across their small TV screens, showing off his good looks during episodes of "My Three Sons"?

For two years, I tagged along as an extra in the Becky and Gloria Act, remaining only as congenial as required without compromising my moral codes. When we walked to school, I trailed behind on slate sidewalks too narrow for three abreast. In class, they sat together in the back corner and passed notes. I sat near the window. When one of their moms drove us to the movies, they squeezed together up front and whispered; I rode in the back, unless, of course, my mom drove, and then I sat up front, and they sat in the back and whispered. At the movies, they sat side-by-side and shared a bucket of popcorn - and whispered about – well, maybe me. I never knew. I bought my own popcorn and sat beside our driving mother of the day.

Their birthdays fell close to each other in late November, and that year their moms bought the two of them the same gifts. The Twins traipsed through the snow to my house to show off what they could wear and brag about what they couldn't. They looked like candy canes stuck in marshmallow in their new shiny red boots and new white, puffy, ski parkas - swishy jobs, with fake white fur bordering the hoods and cuffs, and swirls of red and green embroidery zigzagging around the pockets and down the sleeves. With breathless excitement they boasted about their matching record players – portable, pink, and the matching 45's - Elvis, Little Richard, Fats Domino. They gave each other that secret friend look, that hush-hush, all-knowing glance, the one that says, *We know something else . . . and you don't . . . we're just waiting . . . because keeping it from you is fun . . . and will make you feel left out . . . and super jealous . . . because we're so perfect . . . and we might laugh at you . . . or maybe we'll just keep looking at each other with these smirks on our faces . . . while you envy us.*

Then with practiced choreography, they cocked their heads to the left, shoved their arms out from under their furry sleeves, and said, "Look at th*ee-eeze*," as they flaunted scarab bracelets – expensive ones – 14-karat gold dangles of multi-colored silicone-encased dung-beetles dug from some ancient Egyptian cave, at least that's what their mothers told them, probably in unison.

But the best part, they crowed, was that they got to open all their gifts at Gloria's house. Both families. Together. Everyone oohing and aahing while the matching boxes with the matching wrappings and the matching ribbons revealed the matching loot, on Gloria's dining room table that most likely was decorated to match the one in Becky's house.

At the time, I recognized the ridiculousness of this welded affiliation. I didn't trust either of them a whit, but they were right if they thought I envied them. I was jealous that at least Becky and Gloria had each other.

Once I entered 11th grade, and we all had our licenses, my friendship dilemma diminished as my loyalties shifted and my interests grew. Cheerleading at championship basketball games, a boyfriend on the basketball team, sock hops in Port Henry where I won contests with their best dancers, and a generous, not very professional Algebra teacher, who let us play tennis during class, made the Twins of Westport obsolete.

Eventually, Becky and Gloria drifted apart. I think they got tired of each other. How long can you look at someone else only to see yourself reflected in the other person's skin?

Kristen ended up running away from home after she graduated from boarding school. Becky became a secretary, took up with some guy twice her age, and moved to Florida. Gloria opened a hair salon in Port Henry, called "Absolutely Gloria's," a name she saw in a magazine.

I went off to college, and then on to new adventures, never to be associated with any of them again.

GRATITUDE

Human beings are actually created for the transcendent, for the sublime,
for the beautiful, for the truthful
. . . and all of us are given the task of trying to make this world
a little more hospitable to these beautiful things.

~ Archbishop Desmond Tutu ~

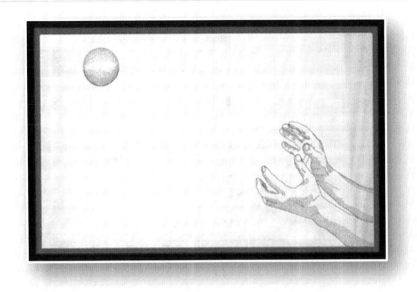

CATCHING ON

Carolyn B Healy

I met Lucia at a writing seminar. She was slight, with a lined, hard luck face and unruly dark hair that obscured her small brown eyes. Twelve of us, all strangers, sat in a loose circle in a sunny high-desert retreat house waiting for the first session to begin. Our leader, a successful and engaging author of personal growth books, arrived and immediately handed out water bottles and instructed us to drink and keep drinking to stay ahead of headaches and any other high altitude symptoms. It was a way of telling us we'd be safe here.

Each of us had a book project in mind and came for help in shaping it into a best-seller. He told us what to expect: Each of us would get two hours to lay out our book concept, the group could ask clarifying questions and provide feedback, and he would provide consultation about how to focus the topic to catch the interest of a large audience. But first, we would get to know each other.

He divided us into pairs and told us to interview each other, and be prepared to introduce each other to the group using one amazing fact learned during the conversation. Lucia and I were a pair. I don't remember the amazing fact, but I do remember that we had remarkable overlap in what our early lives had been like. Both of us grew up only children of widowed mothers living in modest circumstances in a big city; both became therapists; both had two children almost grown; and both had killer book ideas.

As we talked on about our parallel histories, I questioned her about her experience growing up without a father and what she ultimately made of it. My killer book idea was that personal narrative, the story you tell about yourself, has everything to do with how your life turns out and your level of satisfaction with it. And that if you are not satisfied, changing that narrative is the - or at least one - route to transformation.

So how could I not ask? Plus, of late I had been putting an excess of energy into finally sorting out my parental loss and how it figured into my own story, so my curiosity could not be contained, even if it took us beyond the prescribed activity.

Lucia answered, "I remember everyone always saying to my mother, 'Isn't it a shame that you have to support Lucia alone?' 'It's such a shame that Joe left you with such a hard life.' Everything was a "shame." I took that in, and that's how I lived my life for years. Ashamed." She explained that she'd been prone to disconnection and self-pity from girlhood, and had to work hard as an adult to come out of it.

I didn't know what to say, not a common occurrence. I realized that there was a sentence that rang through my childhood too, directed to my mother Jessie: "Aren't you lucky that you have Carolyn?" Or to me, "Your mother is so lucky to have you." Or overheard around relatives' tables, "Thank goodness Jessie and Carolyn have each other." You hear that difference? It was all about luck and good fortune on my side.

I'd long wondered where my disposition toward appreciation and gratitude came from, and originally figured that they must come easy to me because of my early loss. It was no problem for me to tell the difference between an annoyance and a real tragedy that was worth getting worked up about. I didn't need to make gratitude lists to open my eyes. They were open.

I would hear my friends moan about how hopeless and unfair their parents were, and suffer over not being allowed to go on a Girl Scout overnight because they had a family occasion they shouldn't miss. But how do you say something like "count your blessings" without sounding like you're feeling sorry for yourself? So I kept it to myself. I knew what I knew because of my loss experience, I decided, one they hadn't had.

As I grew, I discovered that, as usual, life isn't that simple. And now Lucia further confirmed it. If my original idea had held up, she would have developed the very same practical assessment I had - any day when the roof didn't fall in was a good day. Instead, she had gone through the same loss, but assigned it a different meaning, the opposite one even, and got a quite different outcome.

In fact, the encounter with Lucia proved my new theory - that it's not what life throws at you, it's how you catch it. It fueled my determination to write that book and highlight this route to resilience.

The meaning that Lucia put to her fatherlessness and how I saw mine activated whole different sets of neurons in our developing brains and sent us down entirely different paths. She developed a grim expectation, the opposite of my knee-jerk optimism.

As I look around, what is not to be grateful about? I see others whose attention is drawn to the negative - the latest political scandal or crime statistics or fears about health care or taxes. Happily for me, my attention goes instead toward a dynamite sunset, or a poke in the ribs from a friend, or a good medical report.

Does that make me a Pollyanna, or worse, a self-congratulatory one? Not so. I am lucky, not admirable. I can meet trouble when I see it, but it just can't trump the rest. Dr. Martin Seligman, a founder of the positive psychology movement, asks if the word in your heart is Yes or No, and provides questions to reveal the answer. He rushes to say that even if it is No, there is plenty you can do to nudge it toward Yes, which brings rewards of pleasure, protection against physical and emotional difficulty, and greater achievement. Ask Lucia who worked hard to move in that direction.

My word is Yes. And I'm grateful for that.

One loose end: What about the personal narrative book? I did write up a nice book proposal and an agent friend shopped it around to several likely editors, but no one bit. I'll dust it off one of these days, tighten it up, add my new learnings, and send it out there again to see if it finds a home. I know which story I'm going to lead with.

CANADIAN LANDING

Ellie Searl

Dan slouched over the back of the kitchen chair and twirled salt and pepper shakers through yellowed fingers. Would he pull out a pocketknife and scratch dirt from what was left of his fingernails? He lit a cigarette. Did he take drugs? Drink? His wrinkled, flannel shirt and frayed jeans hadn't seen a washing machine in months, and his scruffy boots would have been thrift-store rejects. Long, greasy hair oozed from the edges of a ratty Montreal Expos cap. The snob in me bubbled over and made me skeptical. But then we couldn't be choosy about who would escort us through this critical event. We either drove ourselves, with our own car, sporting our own license plate, risking arrest, or let someone else drive - someone like Dan - someone with experience sneaking American war resisters back and forth across the Canadian-US border.

It was an underground operation. Dan, a Canadian Aid to Immigration and Draft volunteer, would pick us up at our safe house in Ottawa, Ontario, and drive us across the border into the US at Ogdensburg, New York. There, border guards would question us, and we would lie to them about who we were and where we were going. Then we would ride along the US side, hoping not to run into the police or anyone who might recognize us as war resisters, to another border, and cross back into Canada. At that border, Ed, Katie, and I would enter the Canadian Immigration Office and apply for Landed Immigrant status. On the spot. One chance. If we didn't make it, we'd have to return to the States and face the consequences of the US court system. It was a big deal.

Time played favorites - moving along at a sweet, comfortable pace for everyone else, turtle-crawling for me. My head ached. I felt nauseous. Weary. I wanted to sleep . . . throw up . . . go to the bathroom . . . cry. Just get this day over with.

Ed handled the tension better than I did. He had stopped his banter with our housemates and stared at the kitchen floor, as though the worn tiles held wisdom from previous Vietnam War resisters who had ventured through the unknown territory we were about to enter. I didn't want to push Ed's emotional buttons, so I remained quiet. Only Katie was immune. She played in the living room with her new doll and the dogs. That she might be soiling Raggedy Ann and the red pinafore I had made for her second birthday a month before we left the States was the least of my worries.

"You guys all set?" Dan took a sip of coffee and sputter-coughed.

All set? What was *all set*? Calm? Excited? Ready for adventure? Packed with a picnic, bathing suit, and beach balls?

We headed to the driveway where Dan's rusty green two-door Ford Falcon sat waiting for us. The front left fender, secured with rope and duct tape, heightened my anxiety. Katie riding in this junk heap? I quelled the urge to say *Forget it. I can't go through with this. We'll take our chances and drive ourselves.*

My digestive system spoke for me. Emotional turbulence caused a new cyclone in my belly – and a beeline to the toilet. Katie scooted after me. I let her pull toilet paper off the roll and yank towels to the floor. She made a mountain of white and jumped in it. Her delight in the simplicity of this amusement gave me hope - maybe she won't be affected by all the havoc and instability in her life. Maybe she won't even remember. I felt a little better, changed Katie's diapers, and took her back to the car.

Dan opened the trunk and gave us blank, uncharacteristically clean, white legal envelopes. "Take all your identification out of your wallets or wherever it is, and put it in these - and seal them. All of it. Don't forget anything. And put these in." He took some documents out of a manila folder.

"What's this for?" Ed asked.

Dan rolled his eyes and sighed. He'd answered the question before, many times. "Because you can't cross the border as yourselves. You're going as ... uh ... " He skimmed the papers. " ... John and Martha Smith from Timmons, Ontario." He looked up and handed each of us a credit card, driver's license, library card, and birth certificate.

"When you get to the US border, you're John and Martha Smith. Memorize your birthdays and where you were born. Can't have the border guards catch you looking at your papers to prove who you are." He laughed. "And we'll tell them we're going into the States for the day to ... uh ... to shop. That way it won't look funny if you don't have luggage or anything."

"What about Katie?" I asked.

He tossed our sealed envelopes under some old newspapers and slammed the trunk. He waved his arm. "Oh, just tell them you forgot to bring her papers. Tell them she was born in Timmons. They'll probably be satisfied with that."

Probably? My mind reeled. *What if they're not? What if they catch us? What if ... ?*

"Now, they might wanna search the car for drugs. Gotta expect that. So they could look in the trunk and see the envelopes. Don't panic or make faces or say anything that attracts more attention. They're not allowed to open the envelopes without a warrant. See, that's why they're sealed." He sighed again and shook his head - like he was already irritated that we'd blow our cover. He turned his back to us, walked to the driver's side of the car, and got in.

The harshness of it all. So raw. So real and frightening. Ed must have sensed the burn catch in my throat. He hugged me. "El, it's going to be ok. Don't worry. We'll make it."

All this intrigue. Like a CIA operation for the untrained. Our own personal "Mission Impossible." Would Ed climb through heating vents? Should Katie and I be disguised as circus freaks?

I swiped aside car litter and flopped into the back seat beside Katie and Raggedy Ann. Dan pulled out of the driveway and onto the main road south.

The car rose over the crest of the Ogdensburg-Prescott International Bridge toward the New York side. Below the metal slats, the St. Lawrence River drifted to the gulf and then on into the Atlantic. I thought how restful it is for rivers and gulfs and oceans to have no worries as they venture to new lands and, in spite of logjams or sand bars or drops in elevation, they meander calmly, in relative freedom, knowing their destinations are long established and time-honored. Such peace.

I studied Ed as he watched the river snake around a small peninsula just south of Ogdensburg. Sturdy profile – straight nose, strong chin and cheekbones, hidden somewhat by a short, trim beard. And always a sparkle in his blue-green eyes. Confident. Optimistic. But now his almost six-foot frame slumped against the passenger seat door. He knew it was time.

Dan said, "We're almost at the border. You guys ready?"

Ready? *Hell no* . . . I wanted to shout.

My sweat glands had worked overtime since we started this journey from Ottawa, and blood thumped against my ear drums . Where did I put my fake papers? What was my name? Where was I born? And when? Who was this child – this little girl sleeping soundly beside me on the back seat, lulled by car-sways? I hoped Katie wouldn't wake up when the border guards started asking questions. But then again, maybe she'd charm them into a kind-hearted "Welcome to the States." I dug through my purse to find my wallet.

My dehydrated lips stuck together, and my tongue felt fat. What if this didn't work? What if we were caught? The thought of Ed in handcuffs incited new commotion in my now-empty intestinal tract. Was there a term for dry-heave diarrhea?

"You ok?" I asked Ed. *Stupid question. How could he be ok?* He was responsible for seeing us successfully through this . . . this charade. The impending border inspection was only one of several twists, turns, and possible dead-ends in the maze of our becoming legally established in Canada.

Ed had a way of slowing my frenzied agitation to a steady calm. If my nervousness began speeding down a hill, he'd locate level ground to help the anxiety take a breather. I figured he was fighting his own nerves, but it wasn't in his nature to let them win. "I'm fine, El." Ed smiled. "It will all be fine."

Dan slowed the car to a stop and rolled down the window. A uniformed US Border Patrol Officer bent over and peered in. He looked at each of us – for a second or two longer than necessary, it seemed. What was he thinking? Could he tell? Do our phony identities flash -   Pretense! Pretense!?

Did Ed have *"I didn't show up for induction in the US Army because I don't support the war in Vietnam and now I'm a wanted criminal in America and after we lie our way across this border we're heading back across another border where we'll   apply for immediate Landed Immigrant status in Canada - because Canada, bless its heart, has taken us under its wing . . . "* written on his forehead?

The guard started with Katie and me.

"Names? Dates and places of birth?"

"Martha Timmons . . . uh . . . Smith . . . born in Timmons . . . New Yo . . . Ontario . . . July . . . uh, 1945 . . . . this is Katie, my dau . . . *our* daughter. Born in Timmons, too, in 1968. . . . I forg . . . I don't ha . . . carry them with me." *Jesus what an idiot!*

"What is your purpose for coming to the United States?"

My chest hurt. "Shopping . . . in Ogdensburg . . . for shoes." *Shoes? They don't sell shoes in Canada?*

"And you sir?" He looked at Ed.

Ed was a better imposter. Cool. Unruffled. Level.

The guard settled on Dan. "Sir?"

Dan didn't have to lie, but his demeanor was devoid of deference to authority. He said his name over his shoulder as he mashed the butt of a cigarette into the ashtray.

"Please open the trunk."

Dan got out and walked to the back of the car. I couldn't look. I whispered to Ed that I thought Dan was acting like a shifty ne'er-do-well.

"El - He knows what he's doing. Remember, he's done this before. He's drawing attention to himself and away from us."

I heard the trunk slam shut and the guard say, Move on. Watch the speed limit."

When we finished perjuring ourselves into the US, we entered the second phase of our scheme - getting to the next border crossing without incident. Every person in every car and on every sidewalk and on every park bench was a potential spy, a selective service tattle-tale.

Dan had insisted we stop and eat at some diner in Ogdensburg, stretching time once again, adding more fuel to my anxiety and frustration. I quietly seethed as he savored tomato soup, a grilled cheese sandwich, and fries, Ed managed coffee and toast while Katie blithely munched on peanut butter crackers. I was too nervous to eat.

After the prolonged lunch, we drove along the St. Lawrence River to Massena, a meandering thirty-five miles east. Our car and the river drifted together, it seemed, synchronized in purpose and speed. Each on its way into Canada – each traveling as slowly as clouds moving across the sky on a windless day. At least Dan didn't speed and risk being stopped by New York State Troopers.

Half way across the Seaway Bridge, the song "*Joanne*" came on the radio. Ed hummed along. I watched the ripples in the water and wondered if all this effort, all this expended energy, all our work to establish ourselves in Canada during "*the time that made them both run,*" was just going to end up "*a most hopeless situation.*"

With our identifications back in our wallets, we could at least be ourselves again at the border crossing into Cornwall, Ontario, where the final twist in this life-changing maze would play out – convincing Canadian immigration officials we were worthy of legal status in their country.

We sat in the waiting room for over an hour, distracting ourselves by leafing through French editions of Life Magazines and recently discontinued Saturday Evening Posts. The ads were easy to figure out: Tide Détersif de Blanchisserie, Milky Way Bar de Bonbon, Crest Dentifrice avec Floride.

Actress and activist Candice Bergan graced the cover of the July 24 issue of Life, along with the heading "Dilemma of New Standards – The Draft Board Rules on a Conscientious Objector." I didn't read the article. A few months earlier, we had been stuck on that Selective Service merry-go-round. I knew what the article said. And it still felt like an open wound to recall those months of waiting for the draft board to render a decision about Ed's request for Conscientious Objector status. His request was denied - his religious, moral, and philosophical objections to the war deemed expedient. After all, they reasoned, how could a Catholic promote a liberal, Unitarian Universalist belief system? But then, after Ed's selective service standing was sealed and beyond appeal, and after he received his notice to report for induction into the US Army, the Supreme Court ruled that CO status could, in fact, be granted on moral and philosophical grounds, those very principles that were the foundation of Ed's convictions. Ed was snagged by the Vietnam War net just a few weeks prior to the one Supreme Court decision that could have changed the course of our lives, had the timing been different.

Katie ran up and down the long, dark hallway, trying unsuccessfully to turn knobs on office doors. The water fountain was just high enough and the on-button just loose enough for her to get a good spritz at her face, startling her into gawks and giggles. She was instantly fascinated by this mysterious gadget. I hoped her curious new toy would keep her busy until it was our turn. As long as she was occupied, it didn't matter to me how wet she got. Office workers stooped to tickle her tummy and say hello. She tucked her chin into her chest and swayed with shy delight at the attention - then hid her face in my knees.

I felt a burst of optimism for adventures in an unfamiliar territory. We had an entire new nation to show Katie - and partly French at that. Memories of weekend excursions meandering through the Vermont hinterlands calmed my nerves. Saturdays and Sundays bumping along dirt roads, exploring back woods, eating in small-town diners, discovering better than good bakeries - and just reveling in the magnificence of mountainsides that sloped gracefully into the lush green lowlands dotted with wide-porched white houses, red barns, and grazing sheep, goats, Holsteins, and Morgan horses. I thought, too, about our recent camping trip from Quebec to Nova Scotia and how much I loved the special beauty of the Eastern Provinces. There would be so much more to discover when . . . *if* . . . we were settled in a new home, in a new land.

I joined Katie at the water fountain, got a drink, and wiped her off as best I could. She looked so sweet and normal in her red Stride Rite shoes, lace socks, and that sopping wet, hand-sewn pinafore. I wondered if I'd ever make another outfit for her. Or for me. I loved making clothes – the more complicated the better. My sewing machine was still in our Burlington town house. When would I be back to get our things? And then it hit me – hard. When would *I* be back? Not *we*.

Ed might not be going back. Maybe not ever. Never again sleep in his old, growing-up bed. Never again debate world issues with his parents over pie and coffee in his family dining room. Never again help his dad take down storm windows in spring or put them back up in the fall. If Ed couldn't go back, I probably wouldn't either - at least not very often. The idea of going back home without Ed threatened to deplete what was left my energy.

The Registrar's office door opened, and we were asked in by a tall, red-faced grandfather-type in a white shirt with rolled-up sleeves and an open gray vest. He was friendly enough, and tickled Katie under the chin. "Would you like something to play with?" He gave her a pad of paper, a pencil, and a big, pink eraser, reminding me of simple grade school days.

"Please, have a seat. Only one of you needs to fill out these forms." He handed Ed a pen and a pile of papers written in English and French.

The interior of the office seemed so lackluster - so nondescript. Nothing about it suggested this room was the gateway to a new country. I don't know what I expected – maybe a big sign that said "Welcome to Canada," or maybe a huge Canadian map on the wall behind the desk with a big red pin in it that said "You Are Here" and a trail of green pins saying, "And Here's Where You Are Going." But then this office was just an immigration holding place, where forms were completed and interviews held. There was no guarantee that this was the portal for everyone who wished to live and work Canada. Some were sent back to their homelands.

I watched Ed fill out the forms. So many locations to record for each of us: birth place, first family home, current home, all the homes in between, elementary school, high school, college, graduate school, occupation, other occupations, church affiliation, other church affiliations, and on and on – each with a complete address.

And at the end of every single address, Ed wrote "The United States of America." All over the place - *The United States of America . . . . The United States of America . . . The United States of America.* The forms looked like a crazy quilt of protracted inky tributes to his country. It was as if Ed needed to prove to the Canadian officials that, although he was seeking asylum in their country, he still loved his homeland enough to splash its name all over the application – that he respected his nation, regardless of his desire to leave.

Either Ed was showing remarkable patriotism or he was procrastinating - because as soon as he finished the forms, our points would be tallied - and that would be that.

With two index fingers, the registrar pecked our interview answers on the manual typewriter..

"So, you both graduated from college?" He didn't wait for an answer. He just clicked the keys. "Hmmm, hmmm . . . ok." More typing. "And do you have a place to live in Ontario?" We gave him the address of our AID sponsors in Ottawa. "Hmmm, hmmm . . . ok." Every now and then he flipped the carriage several times in a row, switching to new questions on the form.

Katie sat on the floor folding pieces of paper into little squares, as though she, too, wanted to organize the world into something manageable.

"And what job to you expect to get, Mr. or Mrs. Searl?"

I spoke first. "I can get a job teaching. I'm a certified teacher. I taught in New York, Delaware, and Vermont. And I can teach swimming and canoeing - I have my Life Saver's Certificate. I used to be a camp counselor . . . I'm a really good seamstress . . . " Ed put his hand on my knee and tapped. I stopped.

"That's fine. And you Mr. Searl? What will you do?"

"Whatever I can find to support my family. I'm not particular. I have talent in many areas, and I believe I'm quite hirable." Cool. Unruffled. Level.

Two-Fingered Fred finished his form and yanked it from the typewriter. He looked it over, said a couple of "Hmmm, hmmms," signed it, folded it, and put it in an envelope.

Then he stood up, expressionless, and handed Ed the envelope. My brain lost its balance. Please.

He bent down to Katie's eye level. "You, sweetheart, are about the cutest, most well-behaved little lady I have ever seen. You take good care of your mommy and daddy, now."

He stood back up and held out his hand to Ed. "Congratulations! You are now officially Landed Immigrants of Canada. Good luck to you."

Tears of relief collected in the corners of my nose and made me sneeze. "Thank you, thank you so much," I choked. Did he know he had just saved our future? That my brain had regained its equilibrium? That my anxiety had dissipated and was floating along level ground?

We walked out of the immigration office into the glory of the afternoon sun and over to our friend Dan, who waited for us in his charming, green Ford Falcon, all nicely secured with rope and duct tape.

Katie, Raggedy Ann, and I settled into the comfort of the back seat as Dan pulled out of the parking lot and headed north to Ottawa. I wiped relief tears from my cheeks and thought about ways to sneak Ed home once in a while, Katie played with Raggedy Ann's hair, and Ed scanned our   Live-Work-Breathe-Eat-Shop-Explore-and-Enjoy-Life-in-Canada papers.

I made Dan stop at the first diner.

I was starving.

SOMETIMES WE JUMP

Mary Lou Edwards

"This is not a good idea," I said to my daughter, certain my advice would be ignored.

Her illegal alien friend was handing over one of his many part-time jobs he no longer wanted. That she thought being the delivery girl for Toppi Thai Restaurant was the perfect job for a college student amazed me, despite the fact that I had witnessed many of her imprudent decisions in the past.

"Mom," she tried to convince me, "Pablo says I can make $50 to $120. a night for four hours work. No taxes. I can study between deliveries. This is a very cool job."

"Cool job? Are you kidding? Lia, think about the wear and tear on your car, the teen-agers who will tip you a quarter, driving in bad weather, the horrendous cost of gas, creepy strangers coming to the door, ..."

She didn't let me finish. "Mom, you're being a negative snob. I'm taking the job."

Obviously seizing this opportunity of a lifetime was not my call.

Not a month into this lucky break, she became disenchanted with rude customers, poor tippers, mean dogs, wrong addresses, and kitchen help hitting on her. Just another day in Paradise I thought, taking a pass on the temptation to say *This was your idea, Sweetheart.*

I was intolerant of her complaints, though one day her grievance did send me into high gear.

"Mom," she wailed into the phone, "you won't believe this!"

"Were you robbed? Did you have an accident?" I shrieked, projecting my worst fears. "Are you Ok?"

"I'm fine, but you won't believe what just happened. I walked into Dr. Cannon's office to make a delivery and the receptionist looked at me and started screaming, 'We didn't order Mexican food! We don't want Mexican food!' She went crazy."

"Why did she say that?" I asked bewildered.

"I guess she took one look at my Colombian skin and assumed I was delivering Mexican food."

"You have got to be kidding," I gasped. "That is incredible!"

"I know, Mom, I was shocked too. The lady really went ballistic."

"Lia, what did you do?" I asked stunned.

"I just told her to calm down - that I was delivering their Thai food."

"That's all you said," I probed, offended not only for myself but for my Colombian adopted daughter as well.

"What could I say, Mom? The lady was just stupid."

"Lia, I would have thrown the food on the floor; I would have turned around and walked out, " I said, jumping into my self-righteous, anti-discrimination mode. "She saw brown skin and assumed you were delivering Mexican food? Tomorrow I'm calling Dr. Cannon's office to let her know she has a racist moron sitting at the front desk. The woman should be fired," I ranted.

"Mom, stop. I told her it was Thai food and she settled down."

"Lia, I would have opened the container and dumped it on her desk."

"Mom, that's crazy. Why would I behave like that?"

"Lia, to assume someone is delivering a certain kind of food based on the color of her skin is stereotyping. What would she say to a Black person who was delivering egg foo yong? What would she say to an Oriental pizza driver? Her behavior is outrageous."

"Mom, if she has something against brown skin, that's her problem. Who cares if she's prejudiced? I just won't deliver there anymore. You're over-reacting."

"I am not overreacting. I just hate jerks."

"Then you're prejudiced, Mother, prejudiced against jerks. If I'd known this was going to upset you, I wouldn't have told you. I only shared it because I was so taken aback. The lady is pathetic."

"Pathetic? Your illegal friend probably passed the job on because he'd met one too many Neanderthals."

"No, Mom. Pablo gave me the job because his driver's license expired and he couldn't afford to get another counterfeit one. Did you know counterfeit documents cost a fortune?"

"Lia, I can't even believe we're having this conversation. You're making me crazy. Would you please quit this stupid job?" I begged, smoke coming from my ears. "We'll talk later, I have to go."

I slammed down the phone, desperate to share my fury.

"Why don't you find something else to worry about?" my husband suggested when I related the egregious offense. "Lighten up - it's not illegal to be an insensitive clod," he said blowing off my tirade.

I was incensed by his lack of indignation.

"Lighten up, *lighten up*? You're telling me to *lighten up* when some ignorant wretch slaps our daughter in the face because of the color of her skin? You have the audacity to tell me to lighten up," I shrieked.

"Calm down. You are over-reacting," he said ignoring my pain.

"Overreacting? So you think I'm overreacting, too? You reduce my outrage to overreacting? I could just scream," I proclaimed in my best Bette Davis voice.

"You are screaming, Honey. Don't get so excited. Did it ever occur to you that the woman might be allergic to tacos or maybe was having a bad day?"

"Oh, a bad day, that's a good one - a bad day justifies racism," I seethed. "Maybe if more people took action when they witnessed something like this, maybe if more people stood up . . ."

He cut me off. "Oh, I get it. This is your new action plan - dumping food on the floor. Flinging a piece of moo satay in someone's face is fighting injustice. That is absolutely brilliant!" he declared, eyeing me as though I were an unbalanced bag lady.

"Okay, make fun of me. You know I'm not advocating throwing pad thai in people's faces although, come to think of it, that'd be a novel way of dealing with disparate treatment," I said just to push my husband a little closer to the edge where I was already standing. "Oh, no, now I get it. You're mocking me because you envy my pluck."

"Pluck, *pluck?*" he retorted with an Elvis-like sneer. "Don't you think it a bit strange to make some tactless person's aversion to Mexican food into a hate crime?"

Just then the phone rang.

"Mom, you're not going to believe this."

"Please, Lia, I can't take any more tonight."

"Listen, Mom, just stop and listen. This is the best. You know that Toppi owns Toppi Thai, right? And that her husband owns La Lupita?"

"Yes, I know that, Lia, we've eaten there many times."

"Well, not anymore. La Lupita went out of business last week and Toppi is using La Lupita's leftover bags. When I delivered to Dr. Cannon's office, I didn't realize I was carrying a La Lupita bag imprinted with 'THE BEST MEXICAN FOOD IN TOWN.' The lady wasn't commenting on my skin - she saw the bag," she laughed.

"Oh-my-God, Lia. That is unbelievable. Imagine if I'd called Dr. Cannon tomorrow. She'd have thought I was a lunatic demanding the receptionist's head on a plate."

"Imagine if I'd dumped the food on the floor, Mom, that would have been so awful. I can't believe you gave me such bad advice." Then, going for the jugular, she proceeded, "I think you let your emotions get in the way. You tell me to count to 10 before I act, but you need to count to a thousand," she lectured. "You're too quick-tempered. You're not just a reactor, you're a nuclear reactor."

"I'm sorry. Maybe I did act a bit like Momma Bear."

"Well, just remember, Mom, I look nothing like Goldilocks. She was a blonde."

CELEBRATIONS

*Blessed is the season which engages the whole world
in a conspiracy of love!*

~ Hamilton Wright Mabie ~

ROSE TO THE OCCASION

Ellie Searl

The phone rang at four in the afternoon just after I put the egg yolk glaze on the braided bread dough. It was a guy named Bill. He wanted to check the time of the open house and if he could bring friends. *Thank God. Someone was going to show up.*

I didn't know this Bill, nor his friends, but now at least a couple of people would enjoy my superb hors d'oeuvres and appreciate my style and grace as a hostess. I slid the bread into the oven, poured another glass of wine, and leaned against the counter. I looked at the serving dishes ready for goodies. What was next?

The open house would be the first gathering in our home since we moved to this hellhole of a city in September. I didn't like Youngstown. A steel town. Certainly not a garden spot. Smokestacks belched dirty clouds of iron ore debris. Street gutters ran streams of rusty water when it rained. Back in the humidity and stickiness of July, while Ed had his interview with the search committee, I killed time and tried to cool off in the mezzanine cafe of Strouss, the city's main department store. I looked over the railing at sluggish shoppers moving along the aisles, pawing through piles of tee-shirts, putting earrings up to the sides of their faces, glancing at themselves sideways with a semi-pout, hoping the earrings might make them look sexy. I feared I was going to live in this god-forsaken place and become one of them. I thought I would die there.

The day before the interview, a member of the search committee had taken us for a drive through the park along the Mahoning River, regarded as one of the more attractive places of the region. It was better than the rest of the city, for sure, but I considered all the sights pure ob-scenery. Having grown up in the beauty of the Adirondack Mountains, I didn't want this dreadful confluence of ugliness to be my settling-down place.

I knew the search committee would like Ed, and I knew Ed wanted the job. "There's a lot going for it, El," he said. "It's a city church, and the salary is pretty good for someone like me, right out of theological school. Youngstown is a good place to start," meaning – he'd take the job if offered, and I would have to swallow all the dreams I had about living in a place of beauty.

Ed began his job at the Youngstown Unitarian Church just when a multitude of people needed assistance - spiritually, emotionally, and financially. He signed his contract on "Black Monday" - the very day Youngstown Iron Sheet and Tube, one of the largest steel companies in the world, announced it was shutting down, putting over 5,000 men and women out of work. It was as if an evil force swooped down into the minds and souls of the entire population and dumped everyone's bucket of happiness and economic survival into the river. I felt the demon working close to home - sneering at my misgivings and orchestrating my demise.

With Ed and our nine-year-old daughter, Katie, I became a full-time member of this deteriorating community. Katie settled quite nicely into Youngstown life, never once complaining about the city. She liked her fourth grade teachers and made friends very quickly in her multi-cultural school. It wasn't until she showed me her class picture that I learned who was Asian, Mexican, black, or white. She participated in local activities and played with friends after school. For her, Youngstown was a great place to live.

I knew I had to make the best of it, so I registered in a graduate degree program in counseling at Youngstown State University, began taking piano lessons again after a musical drought, and revived an old lost love of mine - entertaining.

One garden spot of Youngstown was, in fact, my new church. The congregation included wonderful people - artists, professors, writers, musicians, and interesting, everyday people. The church seemed to be a respite from the unpleasantness of the city's decay. And so at Christmastime, Ed and I decided to give them a party.

The dining room table was taking shape. I placed a fresh boxwood centerpiece bejeweled with holly berries and white and red carnations between two silver reindeer with antlered candlestick holders. The table would soon be laden with a cornucopia of sumptuous treats. Poached salmon and lemon slices with sour cream dill sauce. Baked brie en croute with raspberry jam and roasted pecans. Spiral cut honey baked ham and sirloin filet slices for mini-sandwiches on my freshly baked braided egg bread. Miniature spinach and broccoli quiche. Various hard and soft cheeses, stone crackers, kettle roasted potato chips, caramelized onion dip, Chocolate chip cookies, butterscotch brownies, vanilla pound cake with a drizzle of butter icing, cranberry bread and cream cheese. Champagne punch with floating strawberries and circles of pink ice. Special beers and wines. I had plenty.

Guests began arriving a little after five. Soon a low hum of conversation mixed with clinking forks and Gustav Holtz's, "The Planets" filled the rooms, reminding me that being with friends, especially during the holidays, is a gift, regardless of the hideousness of scenery beyond the door. I stood back and smiled at the sights and sounds - lovely table filled with a colorful array of tasty foods; small groups of people drinking, laughing, celebrating the holidays; sparkling decorations for that special touch of Christmas hospitality. Just right.

That's when the three strangers came into the house. Two men and a woman. They didn't knock nor ring the bell. They just opened the door, and with supreme boldness, swept into the room and spread out as if they had predetermined where they would park themselves. The shorter of the two men was dressed in a dark brown and white striped suit that fit him like a flour sack. But it was his slick, comb-over hair, parted so closely to his left ear he'd have to be careful he didn't scratch his lobe that set him apart from the general population. He headed for the living room and stood in front of the fireplace, hands groping the air for warmth.

The taller, hulk-like man slunk into the corner of the dining room behind the door and stood there, shoulders hunched, arms dangling in front of him as though he was about to direct a choir. He rested his chin against his chest and gaped at the crowd from under bushy eyebrows with a dull, menacing glare, like an eagle watching over its prey, ready to pounce. He wore an oversized white shirt under an ill-fitting grey suit that pulled across his stomach, jacket sleeves ending at his forearms, shirt sleeves continuing the journey, falling off the cliffs of his knuckles. His trousers barely made it beyond his calves, landing just above black high-top work boots.

The short, pudgy woman wore black baggy sweat pants that hung out of red rubber boots, ringed at the top with, what probably was, at one time, white fur. Four safety pins fastened over a broken zipper held her tattered hooded sweat jacket closed. A large, white paper Christmas bow, bobby-pinned to her uncombed bronze hair, was placed smack dab at the top of her head. She looked like a forgotten package all wrapped up for the holidays, then stuck away in the closet and left there to collect dust. She made a beeline for the buffet and without pause, began circling the table, scooping food with her right hand and dumping it into her widespread left-hand-turned-plate.

I was at once horrified and fascinated at this turn of events. I was horrified at what I assumed were three city moochers who somehow learned about the meal of the century and came directly from their cardboard box living rooms into in my house to land free food. Yet I was fascinated by the three of them. The bizarre little man in the living room, now examining lint on his jacket. Goliath standing in rigor mortis behind the dining room door. The chubby woman deftly sweeping food from the buffet. Who were these rumpled people? And how did they end up at my fancy party? Should I shoo them away? And if so, how? Were they dangerous? Should I call the police? What were my other guests thinking?

I stared in awe at the expertise the round woman exhibited as she swiftly and magnificently orchestrated her way through each food item, and with pure and absolute finesse, pile it onto her open hand-plate. Across her wide-spread fingers tips she balanced generous slices of ham, sirloin filet, cheese, and bread. Across her knuckles, she set brownies, cookies, pound cake, and cranberry bread. At the V of her fingers she piled chunks of salmon, quiche, potato chips, and crackers. And in her palm, she dumped all the sloppy stuff - sour cream, onion dip, baked brie, and cream cheese. She took a bite of everything as she went. A slice of beef into her mouth, a slice of beef onto her hand. Brownie into her mouth, brownie onto her hand. All around the table. Several times. Eating and piling. Eating and piling. The other guests backed away and gave extra space to this woman whirling around the buffet with such indiscretion.

The president of the congregation sidled up to me. "That's Bill in the living room and Rose here at the table. Don't worry, they're harmless. We all know who they are. They live together in government housing, and they go to everything in Youngstown that has free food. They check the paper for funerals, library meetings, and church potlucks. They must have seen your open house advertised in our newsletter. They're always at our potlucks, but they never bring anything"

Good, I thought. *Who'd eat it?*

"Who's that guy lurking in the corner?" I asked. "He looks like he was built by a mad scientist. I bet he's got wires for brains."

"I don't know him - he's a new one. But if he's a friend of Bill and Rose, he's probably ok too."

I thought about the phone call earlier that had excited me so much and had reassured me that my party would be a success. It had been Bill, this strange short not-quite-homeless man with bad hair who wanted to celebrate Christmas with his friends - just like the rest of us. Bill, Rose, and . . . well, . . . Lurch had come to my party to feel the warmth and joy of the season – just like the rest of us. They wanted to eat, drink, and be merry – just like the rest of us.

Shame slapped my face with a hot washcloth. Who was I to feel superior to three people in need? Was this not an open house? Did I not welcome them before I knew who they were? I walked over to Rose and said, "Here let me help you." I picked up a plate, piled it with food, and handed it to her. "Would you like to sit down?" I led her to an easy chair.

Then I made another plate and took it to the man hovering in the corner. He smiled at me and, without pause, shoved what he could into his mouth - ham, cheese, cookies, potato chips - whatever would fit. I smiled back. He refused my offer to sit down. "Naw," he mumbled. "I like it here."

Bill found his way into the dining room and began filling his own plate. He handled himself with the decorum and grace of a long-practiced buffet-guest. I introduced myself, and we fell into a conversation about adding nuts to brownies.

The hum of the party regained its harmony and rhythm - clinks, laughs, music, and good conversation. It was an open house, after all.

We lived in Youngstown for the next five years, and as much as I continued to dislike the city, I came to love the people – even Bill and Rose, who began bringing a package of English muffins to our potlucks after Ed told them it was important to contribute. We never learned anything more about the guy who hid in the corner.

WHEN YOU SEE
WITH YOUR HEART

Mary Lou Edwards

Dear Lia,

Shortly after Thanksgiving, you sat on Santa's knee in front of the magnificent Christmas tree at Marshall Field's, and you gave him your not very long wish list - a baby doll, a bicycle and, of course, Barbie. You had only been in the United States for six months, but Barbie already was your new best friend.

Daddy hurried to Carmen's Bike Shop to order your first two-wheeler, in part because he couldn't bear to disappoint you, and also, I suspected, because he feared getting stuck assembling a last minute purchase.

"Please don't buy a Barbie bike," I begged as he headed out. "I'm already Barbie'd out."

"I'll look for a Susan B. Anthony bike," he teased, "or maybe one with defiant little fists waving from the handlebars."

"I'm serious," I said. "Girls relate to their dolls, and, if Barbie was real she'd be 6 feet tall, weigh 100 pounds, and wear a 42 FF bra. Lia does not need to be a moving billboard advertising the deformed hussy."

"Oh, stop it. If you feel that way, I'll order a Flying Nun bike," he said, as he kissed me good-bye. "And get shopping before the dazzling damsels disappear from the shelves."

I enlisted Nonna for the attack on Toys "R" Us before the hordes invaded. We found the Happy Holiday Barbie, the Stupid Barbie, the Malibu Barbie, the Doctor Barbie - a few of the many little anorexics you just had to have. Taking a deep breath, I tried to select the least offensive of the idols and settled on Veterinarian Barbie and Little Mermaid Barbie. Feminist that I was, I hoped not to run into any friends who might spot the pert-nosed, Aryan femme fatales in my shopping cart.

"Guard the cart with your life," I said to my mother. These Barbies are hot items. I'll track down the baby dolls." Fortunately, the human-looking dolls were not in such high demand. I found two infant dolls - one for you and one for your sister, Gianna.

I returned to Nonna who was on guard-duty with the Barbie babes.

"What do you think of these, Mom?" I asked, holding up the baby dolls. "They drink a bottle, pee, and cry. Do you think the girls will like them?"

Nonna looked at the babies. "They're adorable," she said, "look at the eyelashes and little bonnets. They're so lifelike," she marveled, "but, Mar," she smiled, shaking her head, *"they're brown."*

"Ma," I said, "Are you kidding me? My kids are brown."

"What do you mean, your kids are brown?"

"Mom, my girls are from Colombia. They're not blue-eyed blondes. They have brown skin," I said, incredulous that we were having this genetic refresher course in the middle of Toys "R" Us while, in the next aisle, maniacal parents fought over the last of the Teenage Mutant Turtles.

"Oh my God," said Nonna. "I never thought about it, but you're right."

I'm right? Now it was my turn to be puzzled.

"Ma, you're putting me on, right? I mean, *you have noticed* your adopted granddaughters have dark skin?"

"Well, I guess so," she said. "Now that I think about it, I must have, but I never really paid much attention. I mean, what difference does it make? Who cares?"

Indeed, why would anyone care? When you see with your heart, you're color blind.

Love,
Mom

MS. CRANKY PANTS
SEIZES THE SEASON

Ms. Crankypants, Guest of Carolyn B Healy

For starters, let me introduce myself. I'm Ms. Crankypants, guest contributor for the month. Carolyn is busy with other things - well, to be honest, I sent her what looked like an official email that the blog was taking the month off so she didn't have to write anything. I don't even feel that bad about it. A girl has to make her own opportunities after all. So this is my chance to tell you what *I* think for once.

About the holidays for instance. I've had it - year after year with the shopping, the decorating, the wrapping, the baking. Well, I don't personally actually bake, but searching the stores for the special cookies that come in the cellophane-covered boxes that are like the ones my grandmother used to make takes a lot of my time.

I'm not the only one who needs a rest. Look into the eyes of your neighbor, your relatives, the shopper who just cut in line in front of you at TJ Maxx, and you'll see not peace and good will but panic. How will she - or you - get everything done in time?

So, I've decided to start a movement - The Christmas Sabbatical. Here's the concept: Every few years you get to take a pass on all the holiday preparations and simply float on top of the season without unwanted fuss and no stress. You become exempt from any expectations. You need to do nothing. Don't tell me you've never thought of it yourself. You have, you just haven't had the, let us say, ova, to carry it out. Or if you have, you've kept it awfully quiet. But don't worry. I'll be happy to take the credit.

I'm starting small this year, just telling a few people like you, my target group - bright, engaged, creative people who have better things to do than fritter away their time on culturally-mandated busywork. I once saw a Martha Stewart magazine where she expected perfectly functional females to waste a day or two of their lives glue-gunning cranberries to a Styrofoam wreath. I know I'm a little bit excitable, but that one sent me around the bend. How will we ever achieve world peace - and it does look like it's going to be up to us girls since the men have been making such a hash of it for centuries - wasting our time like that?

Next year will be the big rollout - a New York Times Op Ed piece, an interview on The View (Elizabeth the conservative one will sputter in indignation), a book deal - but I get ahead of myself. Just to head off Elizabeth and my other critics, I am not suggesting giving up Christmas and what it stands for (which was what? I've forgotten). I just advocate the chance to take a year off from the bustle periodically and see what else shows up to fill the space.

A moment about tone. You want this to be a joyful experience that allows you unprecedented freedom and ease, not a way to bitterly weasel out of your responsibilities. I know to mention this because a certain significant other, call him Mr. Grumpy, I mentioned it to shot back, "Well, don't do it anymore if you don't like it." Which completely misses the point, as usual. Just to be clear: the point is that you may usually love to do all the preparing, gifting, polishing, etc. but after a marathon lifetime of the same, deserve a break once in a while.

And here's the beauty of it - The Sabbatical is not an all or nothing proposition. Given your personality, your budget and your other circumstances, you design it to fit your particular needs.

I have constructed a matrix, elegant in its simplicity, to lay out your options. It is based on first, whether you want your sabbatical to be complete (for those you who have been overfunctioning for years) or partial (if you just want to dial things back to an achievable level). Second, do you want it to be visible (so you can champion the idea) or invisible (so you can use it as an internal guideline to keep your own expectations in check)?

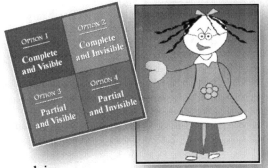

Allow me to explain.

Option 1: Complete and Visible. You just resign from everything you usually do. Boldly declare that you are not participating this year and then duck because there will be a backlash. You will be called an atheist Christmas-denier. Not recommended if you have children in the house. They take everything so personally, and you may scar them for life and I don't want to be implicated for that. I may be cranky, but I'm not a monster.

Option 2: Complete and Invisible. This requires more finesse. You totally take the year off, but don't admit it. Always answer a question with a question, like "So where is the Christmas tree?" with "Have you seen the axe?" You might want to come down with the fake flu on Christmas Eve and get over it on the 26th and watch old movies in between.

Option 3: Partial and Visible. Admit what you are doing with pride. Choose your five favorite holiday activities and do them with gusto, then wrap yourself in the flag of nonmaterialistic values if anything else rears its head demanding to be done. Set an example for your family and friends and recruit them to participate in the big rollout next year.

Option 4: Partial and Invisible. Cut back but keep it to yourself. It will be entertaining to see if anyone even notices what you've dropped, and if they do, if they have the nerve to mention it. Remember to wear your new relaxation on your sleeve, so as to attract positive energy that helps everyone you come in contact with feel like they can settle down too.

Before I let you go to put this into practice, here's a consideration of how the sabbatical concept impacts the prevailing notions about what Christmas must be:

There is the annual scolding that we must "put the Christ back in Christmas," as if it is some sort of religious holiday. This is accompanied by the increasingly confusing squabbles over where people can put menorahs, crèches, Christmas trees, or not. My response: I'll decide exactly what needs to be put in my own holiday, thanks, and you do the same.

And the language thing – can you say "Merry Christmas" to your atheist friends (you do have atheist friends, you know), or your Jewish neighbor or Muslim co-worker, without being an insensitive jerk? This however, requires that you prescreen any possible greetees for their religious identity so you can place them in the proper category which is potentially rude and unwelcome. My outlook: Let's just all get over ourselves and just be glad that someone wants to greet someone else rather than blow their head off. Jeez.

Every year the Christmas card list forces you to make an accounting of your friends and associates, sadly removing the ones who are gone and scouring your year to see if you've made any new friends at all to add, which is a good thing if you ask me. But the Christmas letter thing, oh brother. Talk about making work for yourself. Now Ms. Crankypants likes a good story as well as the next person, but shouldn't have to sit through a recitation of each mole that everyone in the family had removed this year. Limit it to one page and you won't try your patience or anyone else's. Besides, by next year, we'll probably all be down to just a Tweet and think of all the time that'll save.

Finally there is the problem of the proliferation of traditions that demand to be repeated year after year. Just because you flew to Trenton the last ten years on Christmas Eve doesn't mean you have to repeat that this year. Too much accumulation of have-to's leads to the very problem we are trying to solve – drowning in unnecessary commitments. It would be like never getting rid of your gramophone when you went to stereo, and keeping your Beta video tapes once VHS came in. Or listening to your Walkman in one ear and your iPod in the other. We've got to let the past go to create a manageable present. Mindfulness now, that's what I say.

Okay, I think that's it. Don't tell Carolyn I was here. She tries to keep me under wraps, but she's pretty easy to outwit. I'll be back.

Oh yeah, happy holidays.

READERS' FAVORITES

FROM

LITTLE DID WE KNOW:
MAKING THE WRITE IMPRESSION

Don't take life too seriously.
You'll never get out alive.

~ Bugs Bunny ~

WHAT ABOUT ME?

Ellie Searl

He leaned against the center column of the kitchen porch and looked at me with that forlorn, Eeyore pout. His glass eye roved off to the left while the other one welled up with tears. "What about me? What's going to happen to me?" He shuffled to his Barcalounger and slumped into the sanctuary of sculpted dents. Years of lethargy had molded creases into the grey vinyl upholstery, shaping the dirt-encrusted plastic into the exact contours of his body. The solace of familiarity didn't ease his distress. He rested his head in the depression of the top cushion and moaned.

I never quite understood why Dad wanted his recliner on the kitchen porch. We owned elegant, though aged, white ladder-back rockers and wicker chairs, which graced the wide covered veranda on the side of the house overlooking the lake. But Dad wanted to sit with his Scotch on the rocks and watch traffic in comfort, even though there wasn't much traffic to watch. An occasional car tumbled out of the mountain road beyond our house and sailed down the hill to the little village below. Farmers in rusty pick-ups tipped their hats, and truckers hauling silage honked. If Dad were in a good mood, he'd lift his drink, spilling his cheap Scotch on his pants. Otherwise Dad complained that they should "Slow down!" or "Quit kicking up our gravel!"

One summer evening, while the family attempted small talk over before-dinner drinks, an out-of-towner stopped just beyond our property line to admire the orange and purple sunset, the colors shifting and slicing through the mountain tops past our meadows. "What's he doing? His tires are on the edge of our grass. He's trying to make me mad." And then the excruciatingly familiar suffering sigh: a belabored intake of breath through clenched teeth, followed by a slow, heavily grunted exhale. An exaggerated swig of his drink exhibited finality to the event, like an exclamation point giving authority to his pronouncement.

A 'Fred testimonial' was meant for us to take notice, and it demanded a response. If none came, there was a 'Fred coda,' which took the shape of a loud "Hmmm?" as in "Don't you agree?" Nobody did. Eventually someone broke the silence and tried to show reason, which was actually appeasement: conciliatory comments to mollify Dad until his Scotch could kick in and he'd fall asleep in front of TV after dinner. But in our heads, the small talk became big thoughts - big with stress, big with anger, big with resentment - thoughts that each of us had and shared in private but never dared say out loud in front of our father, or mother, for that matter. At moments like these Mom had her own excruciatingly familiar sigh, only hers was shallow and slightly sing-songy, as though she had just seen a baby bird fall out of its nest – helpless and pathetic. But true to form, she'd fake a laugh and say something witty to lift the melancholy that hung over us like a sunset gone to seed.

Dad had a college degree in civil engineering; he was a skilled land surveyor; he showed artistic ability in oil painting, sketching, map-making, and embroidery. He cultivated beautiful gardens with lush string beans, sweet beefsteak tomatoes, and exceedingly huge zucchini. He enjoyed baking bread and making German spaetzle noodles with sauerbraten, and in the summer, he'd husk corn. So what happened?

Dad was a personal contradiction wrapped in a heavy-set, six-foot, three-inch bulk of a man, whose central belief of life and how it should treat him stopped developing when he was in those self-centered teenage years of supreme narcissism. At sixteen, the Me First syndrome is expected and humored. At any age beyond twenty-five, exhibiting childish, self-absorbed behaviors is an embarrassment. Dad was stuck in the expectations of teenage-ness, looking toward others to fill his bottomless happiness glass. That's it. Mostly he just liked to be waited on.

For Dad, being waited on meant guessing what he wanted and getting it for him before he knew he wanted it. His adolescent self reared its head during these gimme gimme episodes. There was hell to pay if Dad saw someone with a treat and his TV tray was empty. "Is that ice cream?" He'd ask in his half-sleep, half-sober whine. Then came the follow-up grievance call. "Can't a guy get a dish of ice cream around here?" Not a proper request that showed a touch of respect, but a command designed to corral the nearest family member into action. When it was my turn, I addressed the situation in silence: stomach in knots, head pounding, face twisted, and hands scooping ice cream into a bowl for the head of the family lazing torpidly in the beige, tufted den recliner while he watched TV with one glazed eye and yelled "Oh, for Pete's sake," if the music got too loud.

When the world behaved properly for Dad, life for the rest of us paced along smoothly. So, to the extent that we could, my two older brothers and I provided opportunities to orchestrate good cheer and lighthearted humor, no matter how emotionally counterfeit the efforts. Pretense was a matter of course. "Make him laugh, and keep us happy." That's how we functioned. We praised his freshly grown vegetables. We complimented his homemade bread, spaetzles, and sauerbraten. We made dinner table jokes that corresponded with something he liked. The jokes became traditions. Dinner was calm if we had rice. "Rice is nice." Dad was particularly partial to that one. It matched a rice commercial that made him laugh, and referring to it meant we cared about him. So simple, yet so therapeutic.

Peace at the dinner table took an ugly turn when the phone rang, or the meat was tough, or my brother's best friend, Tim, came to the kitchen door. "Why the hell does he always have to show up at supper time?" Then, stomach in knots, head pounding, face twisted, and hand clenched onto my fork, I'd finish my meal in agitated silence. Dad sighed his insufferable big sighs, Mom sighed her pathetic little sighs, and my brothers and Tim ate dinner in the den.

Children aren't equipped to understand or analyze their parents' behaviors. I knew Dad had a terrible accident during a wood chopping incident in his early thirties when an errant piece of tree bark flew into his left eye, blinding it instantly. Dad used to complain about his lack of depth perception, but other than that, I never gave his eye much thought. I was used to it. I also knew that Dad was an only child who had been doted upon by his mother and bullied by his father.

Perhaps Dad's disgruntled behavior was due to his ill-fated, debilitating experience. Or perhaps he lingered in those coddled, only-child stages of youth, waiting for a mother figure to lift all stress and anxiety from his world, and still seeking approval from some non-existent supportive father figure.

Whatever the reason, he was rendered helpless. Dad couldn't meet the ordinary challenges of finding fulfillment or gratification in everyday occurrences. He couldn't overcome the all-encompassing hopelessness that continued throughout his lifetime - a lifetime spent drinking Scotch, earlier and earlier each day, letting his garden wither and his artwork dwindle. Did he ever notice that he had three beautiful children, a generous, although submissive wife, and a great deal of talent? Did he know he became an unlovable man?

When I still lived at home, I never confronted him – ever. I was too afraid – afraid of his intermittent love-hate affair with the world he built around him and us. Afraid of his unpredictability. Afraid of his ambiguous, yet omnipresent disapproval that interrupted the equilibrium I tried to grasp and manage in his presence. Whose responsibility was it to build our relationship? If it was mine, I failed. If it was his, he failed.

And so at his worn-out age of seventy-two he wanted to know what would become of him. How would he manage? There he sat in that hideous lounge chair, swirling his Scotch, spilling it on his pants, looking pitifully at the porch floor boards wondering who would take care of him now that Mom had her arm in a sling because she ripped her rotator cuff playing golf. What a sad sight. He'd never change.

But I had. I had found courage. No stomach knots. No head poundings. Nothing clenched. Just a few words forming along with a twisted smile. I couldn't resist.

"Lighten up, Dad. You still know how to pour your own Scotch."

I turned and walked into the kitchen, letting the screen door slam behind me. I have no idea if he sighed or what he said, if anything. It didn't matter.

MEATBALLS ON BITTERBRUSH

Ellie Searl

It's remarkable what an aroma can do. Just a whiff of Italian cooking takes my thoughts across the country to a little spot of heaven and a life-changing adventure in the Pacific Northwest. My journey started at the curb of Seattle's United Departures where Dick and Carol handed me the keys.

"Call us if you have trouble. Don't forget - you'll be out of cell range and radio reception once you start up the pass. The instructions for Sirius are in the glove compartment. Have fun on your adventure, Kiddo. The kerosene lamp is always full. Help yourself to the rum in the freezer. Do you remember where the generator is? . . . Watch out for the deer . . . and the hunters. Wear red."

The groceries purchased at a little IGA rattled around as I drove toward the mountains. I should have packed better, but I was in a hurry to catch the last sharp images of the waning October afternoon. Bottles collided with each other and against my suitcases. The pungent odor of deli peppers and dill pickles filled the SUV; I hoped sloshed drippings weren't saturating the carpet.

I meandered up the winding roads on the west side of North Cascades Highway toward Washington Pass. Autumn splendor dotted the landscape with copper and rust. Shafts of sunlight streamed through splits in the valleys. I stopped at look-out points to photograph breathtaking golden panoramas. The intense clarity of the late October afternoon made this one-woman-adventure-into-the-wilderness exciting and celebratory.

I was on my way to house-sit Dick and Carol's isolated cabin in the mountains while they sailed in the Caribbean. Their Golden Retriever, River, had been placed in a kennel, so I wouldn't be required to dog-sit as well. One time I dog-sat for my other brother's two dogs, and after that, dog-sitting was about as agreeable to me as swimming in oatmeal. Even though there would be one dog, not two, and even though River wasn't deaf and blind, didn't ooze puss from his eyes, didn't need eye drops, didn't take four varieties of pills wrapped in bread - or stuck in peanut butter - or mushed into soggy dog food, and didn't chase around the pool yelping at swimmers, I still refused. I did, however, agree to take care of the cat, Cricket, despite the fact that she was deteriorating from old age and a weak kidney. I knew that Cricket was afraid of people and wouldn't show her face until I had moved around the cabin for at least four days. And cats, sick or not, take care of themselves – as long as they can locate their food, water, and litter box. She was my kind of companion.

I took too much time admiring the changing colors of fading daylight. When the sun finally slid behind the stillness of Lake Diablo, dusk, combined with looming mountain shadows, made driving menacing. The lack of guardrails at outcroppings floating over vertical drop-offs swept away the casual security I had felt just a few hours earlier. I was nervous. The smell of onions, garlic, and pickle juice was strong and nauseating. By the time I crested Washington Pass and started down the steep-graded s-curves, it was pitch dark. The SUV veered around twists in the highway just a few feet from precipitous ledges that hovered over sharp drops to the valley floor.

I rounded the bend where, according to my brother, some kids careened to their death because they weren't paying attention. As excited as I had been by the exquisite views a few hours before, I couldn't look. I clutched the wheel and kept my eyes on the road. Headlights beamed on red and brown where evergreen should have been. The dull colors were out of sync with postcard prettiness. A sense of doom magnified my already waning excitement, and I worried that global warming and infectious diseases were destroying the pine forests of the Pacific Northwest. I began thinking that my venture into the unknown was not such a bright idea. Perhaps I shouldn't have left the company and comfort of my husband and home in Chicago to sail out on my own to this god-forsaken, desolate place. Not even the trees knew how to stay alive.

After convincing myself that those unfortunate dead kids were brainless blockheads on a drunken binge, I navigated the curves with invented courage - easing and braking, easing and braking - down the east side of the mountain, along the river, and then finally, up a steep rise to the safety of the cabin on Bitterbrush Road.

The night was eerily quiet, except for the stones crunching under my feet and a slight swish of branches high over head. Ebony stillness surrounded me. A symphony of stars in sparkling constellations I couldn't name shone on me with mysterious silent glory from an inky sky. Gentle breezes nudged pine needles and oak leaves into singing their tree-songs. Cool air carried the scents of spruce and cedar.

I entered the warmth of the cabin and the joy of my brother's life with Carol. I found a welcome note and house instructions beside a red and white striped bowl filled with Bombay Sapphire gin, Martini and Rossi dry vermouth, a jar of olives, and a cut-crystal cocktail glass. The greeting was sweet and gracious. I placed the martini makings on the painted pine hutch next to the already-flowering Christmas cactus. Night magnificence, forest calm, and cabin lamplight revitalized me after that long, unnerving drive over Washington Pass in the dark. I opened a bottle of champagne, drank a toast to my journey, and with glass in hand, searched for Cricket among the nooks, crannies, and quilts of her home.

In the next three weeks I would go to the farmers market in Twisp and buy sunflowers and home-made, orchard-fresh peach pie from the 85-year-old woman who baked it, pastries from the Cinnamon Twisp Bakery, and double-churned ice cream from Sheri's Sweet Shoppe. I would visit the Winthrop Art Gallery and watch glass being sculpted into vases and bowls. I would drive along the Columbia River and marvel at the immensity and grandeur of our world, and with a packed lunch, take a four-hour sight-seeing boat trip up glacial Lake Chelan to Stehekin outpost. I would sit on the back porch in the rain and work on the New York Times Sunday crossword puzzle, and watch humming birds quiver around the feeders when the sun came out. I would find a Washington Mutual Bank in Omak, 40 miles away, and get my nails done on the same trip. I would congratulate myself on not reaching a state of panic when I woke up at 2:00 am and thought I was blind because it was so dark that it didn't matter if my eyes were open or closed. And then I would scramble for a flashlight in pitch black terror and phone the electric company to ask if there had been a power outage.

I would stroke Cricket, who found me sooner than four days after my arrival, and who sat on my lap and purred despite her fear of humans. I would tend Cricket as her health declined and sadly caress her on her final days and feel her soak up all the love I could give her in her last home under the majesty of the Cascade Mountains. I would take her to the vet and stand beside her and hold her as the difficult but necessary decisions were made to relieve her of her pain and misery. Then I would drive back to the cabin with an empty cat crate knowing that Carol's buddy of 17 years would not be there when she returned home to sneak up on her and snuggle again.

I would read books, write in my journal, walk along the river, drink champagne, sleep when I felt like it, and wear red. I would create savory meals while sipping martinis or white wine bottled in Wenatchee. I'd make fresh vegetable soup and seared ahi tuna with asparagus and BLT's with fake bacon, and an abundance of scrumptious baked Italian meatballs, so many meatballs that I'd eat them again and again with spaghetti or as hot sandwiches or just plain cold, straight out of the refrigerator.

I would stand on the mountainside and look down along the green and orange vastness of the Methow River Valley and thank my lucky stars that I had this opportunity to live here by myself for a short, beautiful time. And I would forever treasure these moments of my journey into self-hood, self-discovery, self-sufficiency, and self-appreciation.

When my senses detect even a hint of oregano or basil, this memory wafts over me and takes me to that little cabin on Bitterbrush where I rejuvenated my soul.

PASS THE PSYCHO-BABBLE, PLEASE

Ellie Searl

Early in our marriage, whenever my husband and I disagreed, we'd argue to the point of verbal warfare.

There'd be name-calling, accusations, recriminations. Issues became cosmic. It took days to get beyond the bitterness and resentment.

I started many of the arguments masking my agenda in a cunningly intoned *"Can I ask you a question?"* This would set Ed's teeth on edge and put his guilt reflexes into high alert. He had learned that this question was a loaded opener - the precursor to kick-in-the-gut combat.

I admit it was weasely to start trouble by asking permission to ask another more accusatory question. I reasoned that hinting at a transgression gave Ed just enough lead time to marshal a generic defense, eliminating any need for a fight - *"Oh, I'm sorry for* (fill in the blank). *Did that cause a problem for you?"* Aside from this blame-eating reply, there were few responses I'd accept. He was wrong. I was right. Ed resorted to sarcasm, and I'd admonish him, tossing in belligerence and scorn for good measure. We became trapped in cyclical point–counterpoint condemnation.

These lose-lose fights left us exasperated and confused. Once we stuck pins into each other's balloons, we didn't know how to fix the holes. I'd develop a headache. Ed grew silent, very silent. It wasn't good. We needed a change.

It was during the late 70's - that period reeling from the aftermath of the Vietnam War - when Ed and I discovered improved ways of communicating. Our country was beginning to heal its civic wounds in the wake of national unrest. Conflict resolution and sensitivity training promoted by peace-not-war Flower Children trickled into the households of mainstream America. Haight-Ashbury hippies roused from their stupors, studied win-win communication, and sought employment with family health plans and retirement benefits. The Civil Rights and Women's Movements gained momentum, causing society to rethink the consequences of inequality, stereotyping, and sexist language. I-messages became popular. And we discovered the benefits of Carl Rogers' Client-Centered Therapy.

This non-directive approach to counseling entered our lives through a series of classes we took for our graduate degrees. Client-centered therapists aren't manipulative. They ask very few questions, and they don't tell their clients what to do, what to think, what to change, or what to believe. We appreciated that people in client-centered therapy could retain their dignity while focusing on uncomfortable issues such as hating their fathers or feeling inferior to their children. It was bad enough that people had to admit they were nuts. They shouldn't also be subjected to the intimidating strategies of an aloof psychoanalyst, writing interpretations on a notepad, making diagnoses, and offering condescending treatment plans based upon coerced answers to embarrassing questions. *"Hmm, mm. And how spastic are your bowels during these times of stress?"*

Ed and I realized we were pseudo-psychologists in our day-to-day relationship, scrutinizing each other, as though studying rat behavior in a lab maze. We interpreted and diagnosed. We bullied each other into acknowledging transgressions, and I connived my way into heart-to-heart I'm right - you're wrong squabbles. But within client-centered therapy and a compilation of win-win, conflict resolution, sensitivity training, non-stereotyping language, and I-messages, we found a bag load of resources to help us devise a new approach to everyday conversation.

We created a home-based, spouse-centered system of communicating. We'd respect each other's points-of-view. We'd keep our emotions stable, our feelings balanced. Our differences of opinion would be settled through negotiation, compromise, and productive decision-making. We'd be in Talk Heaven.

There were ground rules. No angry outbursts. No recriminations. No telling the other what to think or how to behave. No guilt trips. No accusatory questions.

Keep it win-win.

So it began.

We Acknowledged Feelings through I-Messages

"I feel a little annoyed when the driver's seat isn't pushed back after you drive the car."

"I hear you, Ed. It sounds like your legs might get all scrunched up. I don't mean to cause you discomfort. I'll be sure to remember next time."

"Thanks, Sweets. I'm glad you understand."

We engaged in Positive Discourse through Mutual Respect and Understanding.

"I feel somewhat neglected when you watch your favorite shows all night."

"I hear you. It's good to know how you feel about my channel selection. When this program is over, let's pick something to watch together."

"Okay, Hon. I'll read for awhile."

We implemented Reflective Listening Strategies.

"I feel just a tad frustrated that we're moving so slowly down each aisle."

"I gather you'd like me to stop reading the labels. I'll try to speed up."

"Great, and to be honest, I kind of know how much sugar I'm ingesting."

Feelings became clear ...

"I feel really disappointed that you didn't come into the store with me. I could have used your help."

"Got it! I see it disturbs you that I might find it more enjoyable to listen to the radio in the quiet of the car instead of traipsing through the store with you again."

"You seem to understand. I hope you listened to something really enlightening while I did all the shopping and lugged all the stuff."

... very clear ...

"It aggravates me that we came for a dinner party, and now we're listening to some pitch to give money. I must have missed something in the invitation."

"I hear you. Apparently this fund raising event upsets you."

"I should have stayed home."

"Good idea. Go home."

... crystal clear.

"Look, it pisses me off when I choose a god-damned station and then you go and switch the god-damned station to some other god-damned station that I don't want to listen to. I'm doing all the god-damned driving."

"I hear you.

"Of course you hear me, unless you've got shit in your ears."

Sometimes, abject failure tickles the soul.   In recognition of the ridiculous, a giggle rose from my gut and burst through the grin I couldn't suppress.   Ed snickered.   And then full-blown, cleansing laughter washed away the grit of our psycho-babble.

We had been trying to strengthen our marriage by solving problems of the heart with intellectual gibberish and text book terminology.   Our spirits had become lost in a quagmire of artificial I-messages and contrived reflective listening exchanges.   Attempts to follow the rules had made us automatons - following a stoic script written for witless actors.

We missed our intimate relationship with all its foibles and emotional turmoil.   It was time to revisit good old arguing - with some modifications.   We reorganized our new-fangled strategies, separating pitfalls from benefits.   Dump insipid collaboration, keep negotiation and cooperation. Dump gravity, keep humor.   Dump pretense, keep truth.

Now, when Ed and I have a concern, we get right to the point.   I don't start arguments with a sneaky *"Can I ask you a question?"* and we don't pretend everything is hunky-dory when we'd rather wring each other's neck.

NO LONGER WORTH LIVING?

Carolyn B Healy

I slid into the pew. It was a Tuesday night and I went alone. There were about twenty of us, an assortment of silver-haired elders with a smattering of younger people like me, one still dressed for the office, most more casually, as if they'd stopped in on the way to the grocery store. Each of us carefully avoided eye contact with the others.

In the back, a table was covered with tall stacks of pamphlets available for a small fee, "The Right to Die," "Special Issues in Alzheimer's Disease," and other titles. The stacks were so high that it suggested a miscalculation – either another hundred or so people had been expected, or each of us was to grab multiple copies to pass out to our friends and neighbors. In either case, it made the evening seem like a failure before it even began.

The three speakers whispered together in the back of the room, watching the clock. At exactly seven-thirty, the tall lanky mid-forties man in jeans and a plaid shirt strode to the front, while his colleagues slipped into seats in the first row.

He discussed the founder, a British journalist who had assisted his wife, at her request, to end her suffering from bone cancer by brewing her coffee laced with deadly medications. When his career later brought him to the States, he and several others, including his second wife, founded the Society in 1980 in his garage in California, to bring the "hopelessly ill" news of their right to practice "self-deliverance" and of methods to achieve "hastened death."

The next speaker was the stocky kindly-looking woman, gray-haired and dressed like Kathy Bates in Misery. Her voice was strong as she presented the public affairs angle. As she covered court rulings, right-to-die legislation and subsequent legal challenges, her outrage grew. She spoke against the restraints on people who simply wanted to determine their own time and manner of death, and the penalties for those who might assist them.

When she got to the part about famous snuff-meister Dr. Jack Kevorkian, the defrocked doctor who claimed to have assisted 120 people to die, her conviction that he was a martyr to the cause leaked out among her facts. The first death he helped accomplish was a fifty-four year old woman who had Alzheimer's. His last was a lethal injection provided in 1999 to a fifty-two year old accountant with ALS, which led to his conviction for second degree murder.

I set the pamphlets down next to me to give me some distance from heroes who bring death to your door. I had a client once whose religion taught that bad spirits attach themselves to objects, and won't go away until the objects are discarded, or better yet, destroyed. The issue that had brought her to counseling was guilt and anguish that had plagued her for months after the end of an illicit relationship. She proved her theory - all her symptoms evaporated as soon as she burned the notes and trinkets left over from her lover. If she was right, these pamphlets might sweep forces into my life I wouldn't be able to control.

The third speaker, the calm man dressed in chinos and a buttoned-down shirt, outlined the practical assistance system. The wanting-to-die person, while still of sound mind and body, explains his reasons for wanting to end it all. If he passes muster, convincing them of his seriousness and emotional health, he is assigned a guide, a volunteer who promises to stick with him throughout the course of his illness, continuing to discuss the conditions of mind and body and intention. The Society becomes the last matchmaker you'd ever need.

Questions bombarded me. Who are these people, these guides? Survivors of a parent's excruciating death by cancer? Anarchists looking for the cracks in the social order? Well-meaning humanitarians? Libertarians looking to kick government out of our personal business? Does it even matter what their motives are, as long as the person who wants to die gets to? Is wanting to die enough?

The lecturer, a serene man who wouldn't worry you a bit if he sat next to you on the subway, laid out the long-recommended method of - well, since they refused to call it suicide-hastened death: a particular cocktail of medications that could easily be prescribed by a sympathetic doctor over time and stockpiled for the final day. They would then be crushed and mixed into applesauce which the individual could feed himself. If he could feed himself.

A newer method was gaining support as well, he explained, that involved helium and a plastic bag over the head, secured with rubber bands or panty hose. The hope was that this method would provide a reduced chance of unintended survival.

Had the woman sitting next to me sucked in her breath at that revelation, or was that me? There seemed to be too little air in the room, too little movement to account for twenty-some living creatures.

As one who has spent a career trying to stand between suicidal people and their permanent solutions to temporary problems, I had negotiated dozens of deals, even written them down so my client could sign them, "no harm contracts" they are called: "I won't act on a suicidal impulse unless I call you/go to the ER/call the hotline." What an optimistic endeavor, to make rational agreements with people subject to irrational and overpowering impulses. I sometimes wondered if I helped keep people alive by tipping them off to how devastated I would be if they did kill themselves. Maybe the point is to know that someone cares that you are still here, that your counselor is awake at two a.m. hoping that you haven't pulled the trigger.

But this, it began to dawn on me, was entirely different. These people had permanent problems, terminal ones. It also became clear to me that while the suicide decisions that I had tried so hard to prevent can teeter on thousands of precarious and temporary impulses, the decision necessary to a end a life as the Society laid it out is made day after day, over a period of time, and involves planning and long-lasting intention. And courage. And help.

My neighbor offered me a mint. I accepted. A few audience members spoke of their own situations - a spouse with a painful disease, a parent who had asked their help - most did not.

Meanwhile, across town, my mother sat, watched over by assisted care staff. She was at once no longer herself, yet unmistakably and indelibly who she had always been, in the moments when she would still surprise me with a joke or gaze at me with undiluted love. When on earth would her moment have been, when she would have thrown in the towel, declared her life no longer worth living? Should I have asked her that? We were certainly past it now, a relief of sorts.

She would have been, I told myself, of two minds: she would support the right of a person not to live out her days in dependency and diminishing faculties. But she was also one to let things run their natural course. She would survive as long as she could because life was good and she was part of it. Realizing that, I could breathe easier.

As I stood to go, I looked again at my neighbor and smiled.

"Good night, dear," she said. She patted my hand and stepped into the cold night. I folded my handouts and followed.

WRITING THE BOOK ON PICKY EATERS

Carolyn B Healy

Some people remember certain classics from their childhood bookshelves - *Black Beauty, Green Eggs and Ham, The Velveteen Rabbit.* For me, it's the little-known *Cheese, Peas and Chocolate Pudding* by Betty Van Witsen, last published in 1971. It tells the story of a little boy who would eat only those three foods and nothing else. Thanks to my mother I heard it hundreds of times. When I get hooked on something, I stay hooked. At least I was until I joined the *Weekly Reader* Book Club and got started on *The Pink Motel, No Children No Pets, Leader Dog* and the like. And then Nancy Drew came into my life and I put childhood things aside.

By the time I needed it again, *Cheese, Peas and Chocolate Pudding* was long gone, out of print and available only in my memory. One miraculous afternoon in a pediatrician's office, I found a copy in a stack of tattered children's books. I persuaded the receptionist to let me take it home overnight to copy.

Unlike *Catcher in the Rye* and *Dick and Jane*, which I have re-read with disappointment, *C,P and CP* held up over time. (SPOILER ALERT: there are currently no copies available on amazon.com, but just in case you experience a serendipitous discovery like mine and get to read the book on your own, you may not want to read the rest of this paragraph.) It had tension - earnest parents try to get him to eat. It had drama – he sits under the dining table refusing dinner. It had climax and resolution – a scrap of his older brother's hamburger drops into his mouth and he finds it delicious. And it had realism - after that, he only eats cheese, peas, chocolate pudding and hamburger.

In a twist that suggests that the universe has a sense of humor, I gave birth to that little boy in real life, in the person of my daughter Katy. While gobbling her way through boxes of rice cereal and jar after jar of baby sweet potatoes, she spit out all meat products and anything green. As a toddler, she graduated to a monochromatic diet of grilled cheese, macaroni and cheese and applesauce. No candy, no cookies, no meat, no frills. I could have written a book. If the term picky eater didn't already exist, I would have had to coin it.

It wasn't that she didn't experiment some. She liked fish sticks until she found out that they were made of fish; same with tuna salad. She was briefly willing to try hot dogs as long as they touched nothing else on her plate, until someone (I suspect her older brother) told her they contain things like rat lips and cat brains. And she was the only child in America who hated chocolate.

Just like the book, her story has a happy but realistic ending, as she finally ventured out into Grandma's Cheesy Potatoes, cheese pizza and the other Grandma's mashed potatoes and eventually, the occasional pasta and chicken breast. While the color palate remained the same, she could enjoy much more variety.

Once, well into adulthood, that same brother took both of us to an Ethiopian restaurant in his neighborhood. She tried to like it but her revulsion was real and at the end of the meal, she went straight across the street for the biggest slice of pizza I've ever seen.

I have a copy of *Cheese, Peas and Chocolate Pudding* set aside for her once she gets as far as parenting. I know she will bring special insight to its reading.

INTERROGATING MY STUFF

Carolyn B Healy

Last year, my questions were all about why grief strengthens some people and weakens others. Before that, my questions were about how to multitask 24/7. This year, they are all about my stuff.

I used to move at least every five years. The usual young couple-upwardly mobile-growing family thing allowed me to upgrade from college apartment to rented bungalow to older duplex to actual own home. That took ten years, and then began the parade of houses, all of it spanning three towns and another ten years.

Stuff was never a problem back then. Each new place opened up new storage options, so any new item I acquired easily found a spot. Plus, with each move it was easy to jettison the things that had outlived their usefulness. It was a tidy self-cleansing process, kind of a regular stuff enema.

The trouble began 18 years ago just before Christmas, when we bought the current house, an across-town move from a much smaller one. We quickly stashed our stuff, hosted Christmas for the extended family and got on with family life. The next time I looked up, a couple of months ago, I was surrounded, hemmed in, trapped, drowning in extra stuff which occupied nearly every nook and crevice in this once roomy house.

To understand my issues, you have to understand my marriage, a good but not easy match. Without me, my husband would probably prefer life in a sterile box devoid of any decoration save a decanter for his bourbon, a copy of This Old Cub, his favorite DVD ever, and his big screen TV.

Without him I might have inched closer to hoarder heaven. His unwillingness to tolerate visual clutter has helped me contain most of mine to my home office where I covered nearly every square inch of wall space with meaningful photos, my collections of suns and moons, a wall cabinet filled with mementos from my parents' era, and well, you get the idea.

What he may not know and the casual observer would miss is that I also have stuff cleverly hidden in strategic locations elsewhere in the house – in antique trunks and painted chests, under the bed, and under the other bed. Meanwhile, he somehow gained custody of the upstairs closets where he can spread out his wardrobe so that each shirt has breathing space. He didn't pee on the boundaries of his closets, but he protects them like he did. My move was to seize the basement. And fill it. As the years went on, we reached this stuff stalemate until nothing new could enter the house without something old leaving.

We lived like that in relative harmony until we recently decided to redo my office and the room next door, our bedroom, and finally remove the aqua carpeting that had come with the house and the blue paint we had added in our first year here.

Right now, the painting is done, the walls a calm beachy tan color, the new carpet is on order and the rooms are completely dismantled. Which brings me to the point where my questions kicked in.

Carrying box after box, bag after bag and stack after stack out of that office, I had my moment of truth - my stuff was unmanageable. I had to do something different to recover my freedom, my space, my lightness of being. My stuff had taken on a life of its own, like a kudzu vine wrapping itself around everything in sight. I had to take control. I resolved that I would conduct this project like a move, questioning the right of each item to re-enter the room when I move back in.

I started with my books, which are relocating to guest rooms where they will provide a gracious background for visitors. They will have a happier life there on their own, and I can visit them whenever I want.
The rest of the process will be more difficult. The interrogation will go like this. Each item will have to answer three questions to get back in:

1. *What do I need you for?*
- Are you about the past, the present or the future?
- Given that, why do you get to stay?
- Is your appeal practical, emotional, or spiritual? And so what?
- Will I use you never, occasionally, all the time?

2. *What do you say about me?*
- Do you reflect my whimsical side, a sad or serious time, a quality I have, an opportunity I missed?
- What need were you to fill, and do I still have that need?
- How do I feel when I see you?

3. *Would I buy you today?*
- Do you belong with me at this point?
- Is there something else that should have your spot instead?
- Is there someone else in the world who would love to have you more than I do?

Feeble answers like "But you've always had me," or "You'll never make it without me" just won't cut it.

I have two giant boxes, in the basement of course. One will be for donations, the other for my upcoming Museum of Things I Can't Stand to Get Rid Of But Don't Need to See Every Day, another place I can visit if I feel the need. With this plan, I feel better already, sure that next year's questions won't have to have anything to do with my stuff.

My new insight: figuring out which questions to ask when just may be the key to the life we all want. It is now too late, but I see that I could have used a do-over on some of my earlier efforts. Instead of asking how to better multitask, what if I would have explored how to become more mindful 24/7? Maybe that's what's coming next.

ELEPHANTS IN LIMBO

Mary Lou Edwards

Long before learning to read books, I learned to read people. Having a father with a mercurial temperament was the catalyst, no doubt. Being on hyper-alert for glaring eyes, exasperated sighs, raised voices - the phonics of dysfunction - often, but not always, kept one out of harm's way.

A subskill necessary for people-reading fluency was learning not to ask questions. Way before 'Don't Ask, Don't Tell' became a part of America's political lexicon, I'd been trained in 'Don't You Dare Ask' - a skill I so perfected a mere raised eyebrow, a simple sideward glance was enough to stop. right. there.

The list of verboten topics was endless encompassing everything from family history to current events. Further complicating the problem was the fact that no map existed showing where the land mines lay and an innocuous inquiry often detonated an explosion of confusion that neither education nor therapy could heal.

"Dad," I asked as I knelt at the family plot in Mt. Carmel Cemetery, "why are Little Nonna and your brother and sisters buried here while Grandpa is all by himself at Oak Ridge Cemetery which isn't even Catholic?"

"You're supposed to be praying for the dead not asking nosy questions that are none of your business," he said in his usual you-are-such-a-pain-in-the-neck voice as he tried to shimmy the old gravestone the years had pushed off center.

"Mom, why doesn't Daddy talk to Uncle Joe?" I asked, after observing at a family wedding reception that some of my favorite relatives were seated at tables at the opposite end of the banquet hall.

"If you were supposed to know, Miss Nosy Pants, we'd tell you," she answered, staring straight ahead.

Once I was peering through our venetian blinds watching the public school kids walk by on their way to class. My brother, sister and I had the day off in honor of the Feast of the Immaculate Conception. "Why do mostly colored kids go to Ward School and only white kids go to St. Jerome's?" I wondered aloud.

"I suppose because they're not Catholic," my Mother said in a tone of voice suggesting I should be on my hands and knees helping her wax the kitchen floor instead of staring out the window.

Ignoring the hint, I persisted. "Aren't they worried about going to Hell?"

"I guess not. Go do something useful."

"What's in a CONDEMNED movie that makes it bad?" I asked my friend, Janice, as I searched The Motion Picture Ratings in *The New World*, the Catholic weekly newspaper, hoping to find a movie my parents would let us see. "Don't even look at the Condemneds," she warned, "or we'll be in big trouble." Then she added, with cantaloupe-sized eyes, "We're not even supposed to be talking about this stuff, but my aunt said Baby Doll is a dirty movie and that's why it's a C."

After years of "don't be so nosy" and "mind your own business," hundreds of grimaces and rolling eyeballs, I came to believe that not only our living room, but everywhere I roamed, was a veritable elephant graveyard.

Would I never know why Uncle Salvatore lived in a hospital, what Uncle Gio died from or why colored people lived two blocks away but never crossed Wentworth Avenue? Even Nancy Drew, my favorite girl detective, would have been hard-pressed to solve these mysteries with every question stonewalled.

Years later, I could really relate to the rabbi who prayed at the Wailing Wall for a half century with no reward. "What does it feel like to pray for peace at the Wailing Wall for fifty years only to have your country in constant conflict?" he was asked. "It feels like I'm talking to a fucking wall," he said.

I sympathized with the rabbi, but at least he'd never been subjected to the Sister Adorers of the Most Precious Blood. Trained as human walls to not recognize a straight answer, they specialized in teaching a unique blend of God's Word and bizarre folktale.

As a student, I tried very hard to restrict my questioning to only those issues which truly baffled me since these harridans had no compunction about playing the 'God will send you to Hell' card to keep kids in line. There were times, though, when I just really had to take the risk and at least try to get some of this straightened out. I knew I couldn't get to the bottom of everything at once lest I be expelled as a "troublemaker" and shipped to the public school so I'd judiciously drop a question here and there.

"Sister," I asked when she was not on the warpath, "why would God punish a baby and send it to Limbo forever just because she died before she was baptized?"

"God knows what is best for us," Sister said.

"Sister, if your body must be buried in a consecrated cemetery in order to go to heaven, what happens to people who burn in fires? What happens if someone dies in the forest and an animal eats him? Does he go to Hell?"

"Finish your assignment instead of worrying about animals in the forest."

"Sister, what happened to the Christian martyrs who were eaten alive by the lions in Rome? What if the lions left an arm or a leg? Would the arm and leg get buried? Would just the arm and leg go to heaven? Would God say, 'I know all things and I know who you are even without your head. Come on in anyway.'"

"You are making Jesus very sad with all of your silly questions," Sister hissed.

But I couldn't stop wondering and worrying - not just about the Coliseum and the Limbo babies and the forest.

What about my friend Catherine's mother who was getting divorced and going to Hell? Catherine said her mother told her it was better to go to Hell than stay married to Catherine's father. How could anyone, in her right mind, deliberately antagonize God with a statement like that? I could just hear God say, "Lady, you are toast!" I said a novena for her hoping to mitigate God's anger, but boy, she sure was asking for it.

And then there was the boy across the street who was killed in a car crash the very same Sunday he slept through Mass. All the busybodies said his mother set the alarm clock for him but he'd turned it off. Did he turn it off deliberately and say, "The heck with it. I don't feel like going to Mass today." Or did he turn it off thinking he'd just lie there an extra five minutes and accidentally fall asleep? Big difference. If he intended to slap God in the face, he was burning for all eternity. If it was just a stupid mistake, God might have shown him some mercy and he'd just have to make a stop in Purgatory before going to Heaven. How long would he be stuck in Purgatory? Oh, no. I hoped God didn't take that the wrong way - I mean, I didn't really mean *stuck*. I knew Purgatory was a lucky detour around Hell - no one cared if it took a little longer to get to heaven.

I prayed God understood I wasn't trying to be a smart-aleck. I just really needed more answers, but I was getting the message, albeit slowly, that asking made things even more complicated. Maybe I was supposed to stop with the questions and mind my own business. Maybe there were some things I wasn't smart enough to understand. Maybe it was true that if it was in my best interests , they'd tell me.

I asked the priest about it in Confession but all he said was, "Bless you, my child, just believe," but believe what?

Did Father not realize I wanted to believe, but I was having trouble with some things that just weren't adding up?

Then slowly, as I grew up, I noticed more inconsistencies, many contradictions, even some big fat lies and no one said a word.

Why did priests, who took the vow of poverty, drive luxury cars and get new ones every year? Why were our nuns paid $8.00 a month? What happened to indulgences that were supposed to get me into heaven sooner? How was it that the wealthy got annulments while the divorced who had no financial resources were banned from the Sacraments? Why did exorcism vanish? Abortion is killing, but war, well, that depends? What happened to the $4 million dollars that the National Council of Bishops lost when Chicago's Cardinal Cody was treasurer? Why, for over twenty-five years did the Cardinal's divorced cousin with two kids always live across the street from him no matter where he was assigned?

The questions kept coming and they ranged from the ridiculous to the scandalous.

Cardinal George announced at a press conference that the Pope had declared Limbo a thing of the past. "From now on," he proclaimed, "Limbo will no longer be taught."

"Does that mean," an obviously pagan reporter had the nerve to ask, "that Limbo no longer exists?"

"I didn't say that," said the tap-dancing Leader of the Flock, "I said the Papal directive states it will no longer be taught."

Nice turn of phrase - world-class parsing that would make Bill Clinton envious, but, let's be honest, Limbo is so last millennium the Faithful consider George's proclamation white noise.

Let's save our energy, some said, for things that really matter. Does a Holocaust denier qualify?

"In the interests of unity in the Church . . ." the Pope recently UNexcommunicated a bishop who loudly proclaims that no Jews were gassed in Nazi death camps.   After a disastrous two weeks of international outrage, the Pope backpedaled insisting no one told him - the German Pontiff - about this hate monger's horrendous reputation.

Could it be that the world's premier Christian asked one of his sycophants and was not given a straight answer? Or could it be he did not hear the answer because of the trumpeting of elephants chained in the Vatican's dungeon of Dogma?

I'll bet at least two of those Papal bulls, Hypocrisy and Pedophilia, are making quite a racket these days and the College of Cardinals better pray that Complicity does not rear his ugly head too.

NOT A PERMANENT SOLUTION

Mary Lou Edwards

I wonder, if in the Land of Make Believe, these baby dolls have flashbacks about their first permanent wave. I know mine was seared into my brain.

I was about to start first grade. Apparently neither the nightly ritual of winding endless banana curls on my fidgety noggin nor my non-stop whining about stupid boys yanking on my braids was appealing to my mother so her cousin Della the beautician's suggestion of a hot perm seemed like the perfect solution.

Though I viewed the horrendous contraption with its black wire tentacles and gleaming steel curler clamps with great trepidation, my mom said I'd be too busy reading books to waste time on the nightly hair-setting ritual. This permanent, she promised, would end my hairy tales of woe; I'd be permanently beautiful.

It took hours to section my massive mane into appropriate sized chunks for the electric curlers. Only the promise of a fuchsia hair ribbon forced me to sit still atop two giant Chicago telephone directories. Finally a disgusting permanent wave solution was applied to each curler and Della threw the switch.

Immediately my head started hissing and steaming like a pot of boiling ravioli. With her eyes as big as the giant meatballs my Nonna fried on Sunday morning, my mother asked, "Della, is her head supposed to smoke like that?"

"That's only steam," said Della, "If her hair was burning, we'd smell it - singed hair smells disgusting."

Looking at my mother's popping eyeballs and smelling the stinking fumes sent me into orbit. My sotto sobs erupted into what would have been hair raising shrieks had not my head been so wired.

"This is an electric chair!" I screamed. "I'm turning into Frankenstein!"

My mother grabbed the telephone book highchair.

"Sit still," she hissed. "If you fall off those phone books, you'll be scalped like an Indian and you'll have to wear a babuschka to school. Besides," she grinned, "You told me you wanted to be beautiful!"

That was true. I did want to be beautiful. I settled down.

A few minutes later the wires were disconnected, the hair unwound and a nauseating "neutralizer" was sloshed through my ringlets. Then my locks were twisted into pin curls and I was placed under a giant steel helmet for another hour to dry.

At last my tresses were combed out with the coveted fuchsia bow planted in the massive eagle's nest of curls.

I was beautiful.

Two weeks later my hair was stick straight. The beauty maven said the "hot wave" didn't take; she would give me a "cold wave."

"No, no," I told my mother, "No, thanks! No more torture. Being beautiful is way too much trouble." And so it was and it is... .

THE TORTURE HOUR

Mary Lou Edwards

The dinner hour started in its usual manner with warnings of don't touch, it's hot, be careful. Mom placed a Pyrex platter on the table guaranteed to jump start every salivary gland on the planet. Wisps of steam rose from the bubbly gravy and stringy mozzarella smothered yet another culinary masterpiece. It was hard to believe that such an auspicious beginning, replete with the heavenly aroma of basil and olive oil, could turn into a meal from hell, but we'd been through the drill often enough to know the inevitable conclusion.

The minute my father opened the cedar-lined closet doors the drama began. Just hearing the creaky wheels of the cart that held the behemoth Magnavox reel-to-reel tape recorder roll over the slick wood floor would be enough to start the nervous snickers and stage whispers to mom.

"Please, Mom," my brother begged, "don't let him ruin our dinner again."

"You know you hate it too," I'd hiss. "Be honest, Mom, and make him stop."

"I'm not hungry anymore," my sister would whine.

"You kids had better be quiet," Mom would warn, giving us a take-no-prisoners look. "Don't make trouble and get him angry!"

By then Dad had threaded the huge circular wheels with the magic music recently captured on magnetic tape and was taking his seat at the head of the table. As we bowed our heads for the requisite murmuring "Bless us, O Lord, for these Thy gifts . . ." we knew the amen would signal the beginning of the torture hour also known as the music appreciation lesson. In reality, it was the precursor to waterboarding.

Even the heaping plates of fabulous food could not anesthetize us from the musical cacophony that was to ensue.

With the loud click of the PLAY button, the air was filled with Lawrence Welk leading his band of acoustic terrorists with "Ana one, ana two, ana three . . ." in a nauseating version of the Beer Barrel Polka or his Champagne Lady of Music warbling "I'm Forever Blowing Bubbles."

By the end of the first stanza, the deterioration of the family dinner had begun.

With each grating, offensive squeak of the string assassins, my brother would grimace and clutch his heart as though being attacked, my sister would knock over a glass of milk hoping to get sent to her room, our dog Skipper would skitter off suddenly remembering a prior engagement and my martyr mother would be looking heavenward as though begging God to strike her deaf immediately. My father's steely-eyed glares of disgust at this contemptible conduct elicited more wisecracks and uncontrollable laughter inevitably resulting in the family sin worthy of capital punishment - milk-pouring-from-someone's- nose-who-was-acting-silly!

"It is sinful to waste milk and revolting," Dad would intone and, at this point, the simple dysfunctional family dinner would turn into an event guaranteed to provide full-blown post-traumatic stress disorder.

Snapping the STOP button, he would launch into tirades about rudeness, ingratitude and stupidity interspersed with "You kids don't know good music." His tongue lashing about our being unteachable was rather paradoxical since it was Mr. Welk who would declare, "Myron and I will now do a solo together." After all, we'd know the difference between the Roman numeral I and a capital I on a cue card and wouldn't announce, "And now for a song from World War Eye." but we were the idiots? The irony was knee deep but totally wasted on my dad who'd pontificate, "They don't write songs like this anymore . . ." as "Mairzy doats and dozy doats and liddle lamzy divey . . . blared in the background.

Actually my father's harangues were more palatable than Welk's prototype elevator muzak. Somehow our digestive tracts had become accustomed to my dad's force feedings of ridicule and shame, but our lower GI's never quite adjusted to the diabetic inducing renditions of "Somewhere Over the Rainbow."

ELLIE VOLCKMANN SEARL writes of human nature - the ordinary and the eccentric - getting to the heart of life's yearnings, idiosyncrasies, and ambiguities. The splendor of the Adirondack Mountains and Lake Champlain seeped into her being, as did the rhythms of small-town life. Her slice-of-life storytelling draws inspiration from rich experiences with diverse cultures, quirky personalities, and unusual encounters while living, working, and raising a family in New York, Delaware, Vermont, Ontario, Quebec, Ohio, and Illinois. Ellie's stories reflect her passion for justice, equality, and freedom of the spirit. She taught the art of writing to Chicagoland middle-schoolers, whose curiosity, energy, and enthusiasm for life gave her insight into the dreams of the sometimes disregarded. When not writing, Ellie designs and formats books. She also creates and manages websites and blogs.

www.elliesearl.com *www.andthenstories.com*
www.writeimpressionstories.com

CAROLYN B HEALY is a therapist-turned-writer who has invested hundreds of hours listening to people as they rewrite their life stories. While her interests include serious things like grief, resilience, and transformative change, her vantage point allows her to address them with insight and a certain dark humor. A lifelong Chicagoan, she grew up the only child of a single mom, which fueled her curiosity about how other people live, and strengthened her backbone. She has been a columnist for her local newspaper and is writing a book on finding the hidden gifts in grieving.

www.carolynbhealy.com *www.writeimpressionstories.com*
www.theinquiringmindstories.com *www.mscrankypants.net*
www.cubacurious.com

MARY LOU SCALISE EDWARDS is a Chicagoan born into an Italian-American Catholic culture with all the richness and liabilities that encompasses. Growing up in Bridgeport, a Chicago neighborhood steeped in the traditions of politics and prejudice, she lived alongside mayors, mobsters, and moguls. At the University of Illinois, she discovered the whole world was not Catholic and the Earth was round. Her writing blends ingredients of domestic impairment, parental missteps, and family complexities with divine irreverence. She then serves up stories stirred by her skepticism and simmered for a lifetime. The reader indulges in a time that was . . . yet is. Mary Lou is currently at work on LETTERS TO LIA: HARD COPIES SO YOU NEVER FORGET.

www.mledwards.com *www.havingthelastwordstories.com*